NEW JERSEY ASK7

LANGUAGE ARTS LITERACY TEST

Joseph S. Pizzo, M.Ed.
Grade 7 Teacher
Black River Middle School
NJCTE Educator of the Year Award 2005

Copyright © 2008 by Barron's Educational Series, Inc.

All rights reserved. No part of this book may be reproduced or distributed in any form or by any means without the written permission of the copyright owner.

All inquiries should be addressed to:
Barron's Educational Series, Inc.
250 Wireless Boulevard
Hauppauge, New York 11788
www.barronseduc.com

ISBN-13: 978-0-7641-4019-8
ISBN-10: 0-7641-4019-1

Library of Congress Catalog Card No. 2007046829

    Library of Congress Cataloging-in-Publication Data
Pizzo, Joseph.
New Jersey ASK grade 7 Language Arts Literacy (LAL) test / Joseph Pizzo.
   p. cm.
Includes index.
ISBN-13: 978-0-7641-4019-8
ISBN-10: 0-7641-4019-1
 1. Language arts—Examinations—Study guides. 2. Language arts—Study and teaching (Middle school)—New Jersey. I. Title.

LB1631.5.P59 2008
428.0076—dc22
  2007046829

Printed in the United States of America

9 8 7 6 5 4 3 2 1

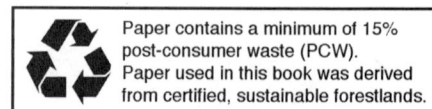

CONTENTS

INTRODUCTION / vi

CHAPTER 1: WRITING A PERSUASIVE ESSAY— 10 STEPS TO SUCCESS / 1

    Major Task: Write a Persuasive Essay / 1
    Pre-writing Your Way to Success / 5
    Ten-Step Strategic Plan for Success / 6
    Independent Writing Practice / 27

CHAPTER 2: WRITING A SPECULATIVE ESSAY— 10 STEPS TO SUCCESS / 31

    Some Key Questions / 31
    Creating a Story Plan / 32
    Independent Writing Practice / 50

CHAPTER 3: READING—LITERATURE / 55

    Use the Preview Techniques (PT) to be Successful / 55
    Target Skills 1-3: Plot, Characters, and Setting / 56
    Target Skills 4, 5, and 6: Theme, Cause and Effect, and Point of View / 66
    Target Skills 7 and 8: Conflict/Resolution and Making Predictions / 75
    Target Skills 9 and 10: Mood and Tone / 86
    Target Skills 11-15: Poetic Devices—Metaphor, Simile, Personification, Rhyme and Scheme, and Alliteration / 96

CHAPTER 4: INFORMATIONAL (EVERYDAY) READING / 107

Target Skills 1 and 2: Details and Sequence of Events / 108
Target Skill 3: Central Idea or Theme / 117
Target Skills 4–6: Questioning, Clarifying, and Predicting / 127
Target Skill 7: Fact versus Opinion / 137
Target Skill 8: Following Directions / 147
Target Skill 9: Recognizing Literary Forms and Information Sources / 157
Target Skill 10: Finding Information and Answering with Prior Knowledge / 167

CHAPTER 5: GRAMMAR GUIDE: USING GRAMMAR CORRECTLY IN YOUR WRITING / 179

Target Skill 1: Agreement—Number, Case, and Gender / 179
Target Skill 2: Misplaced Modifiers / 182
Target Skill 3: Voice / 182
Target Skill 4: Sentence Variety / 183
Target Skills 5 and 6: Fragments and Run-ons / 185
Targets Skills 7 and 8: Punctuation with Commas and End Marks / 186
Targets Skills 9 and 10: Homophones and Homographs / 188
Target Skill 11: Grammar Demons / 190
Target Skill 12: Spelling Demons / 195

CHAPTER 6

Practice Test 1: Answer Sheets / 197
Practice Test 1 / 207

CHAPTER 7

Practice Test 2: Answer Sheets / 215
Practice Test 2 / 225

CHAPTER 8: ANSWER KEYS AND EXPLANATIONS / 235

CHAPTER 9: APPENDIX / 273

Success Tips for NJ ASK 7 LAL
    Essay Writing / 273
Test-Taking Success Strategies / 274
Sample Graphic Organizers / 275
Speculative Writing Organization Sheet / 278
Some Commonly Misspelled Words / 278

INTRODUCTION

As you prepare to take the New Jersey Assessment of Skills and Knowledge (NJ ASK) Test for Grade 7 Language Arts, you probably have a question or two that need to be answered. Before we begin practicing for the test, let's try to answer some common questions that you may have.

What is the NJ ASK Test?

The NJ ASK Test is a test given by the State of New Jersey to all of New Jersey's public school students in grades 3–8. The two subject areas tested are language arts and mathematics. In grades three and four, science is also tested. The practice tests in this book will deal only with language arts.

Do I have to take the NJ ASK Test?

Yes, you must take the NJ ASK Test. The State of New Jersey requires the test so it can determine whether you are learning the proper skills in your classroom each year. If you happen to do poorly, then your school will get you extra help so you can learn all your skills and get a better score on the next year's test.

Does the NJ ASK Test change every year?

The test is a little bit different each year. The writing sections for seventh graders will require you to write persuasive essays. This is the same requirement that is part of the sixth grade test. The writing from a picture prompt section is now the Speculative Writing section for grades 6–8.

Besides the persuasive essay section of the test, what other types of questions will I be asked on the test? Also, are there any more essays?

There are two types of questions in the reading part of the test. The first type of question is multiple choice. You're given four answers and asked to choose the correct one. The second type of question is open-ended. Here you're asked to respond to passages that you have been given. Some of these are poems, parts of novels, or other pieces of literature like fables. The other types of passages may be news reports, parts of textbook chapters, or other writing that's using facts. These passages may have information displayed in charts, graphs, timetables, or lists. You may be asked to use this information to write your essays, in addition to applying your general knowledge (things you already know). These short and long essays are part of the reading section of your test.

How do I answer these open-ended questions?

To answer these types of questions, you'll write both short and long essays. The short essays usually seem to be about 3–5 sentences long (one short paragraph). The long essays usually seem to be at least 4–8 sentences long (one paragraph). If your question needs more information, then you should add a second paragraph.

If I'm a Special Education student with an Individualized Education Program (IEP) or a Student with a Disability (Section 504), do I have to take the same test as the General Education students?

If you're a student who needs special accommodations in the classroom, then you'll receive the same or similar accommodations for the test. If you're severely disabled, then you'll receive the Alternate Proficiency Assessment. If you have limited English proficiency (LEP) because you are just learning English, then your parent(s)/guardian(s) should check with your school for advice.

What's the best way for me to get ready to take the NJ ASK Test?

The best way to get ready for the test is basic. Simply stated, give your mind a good workout every day.

How can I give my mind a good daily workout?

Here are some tips:

- Do your best in school every day.
- Pay attention to your lessons and complete all your homework.
- Practice writing and editing every day, both in school and at home.
- Read for at least twenty minutes a day.
- Before you hand in your homework, always look it over to check for mistakes.
- Limit your time watching TV, playing video or computer games, surfing the Internet, sending text messages, and listening to music.
- Get enough sleep every night, especially on nights before a test.

When I finish all of the exercises in this book, will I be guaranteed to pass the NJ ASK Test?

Unfortunately, no book can make that guarantee. If you are serious and you complete all of the sections in this book carefully, your chances to do well on the test should increase. Please remember to review any sections that you find to be difficult ones.

As you work through each section of this book, be sure

- to make a personal vocabulary list of any words you don't know.
- to turn off your phone and get rid of any distractions before you begin each exercise.
- to put away all snacks that are crunchy or messy.
- that if you take a break that it is a short one.
- to practice the sections that give you the most difficulty.
- that if you find a section of the test that is really giving you problems, that you ask your teacher for some extra help.

Good luck on your test!

RUBRIC

On the following page is a copy of the rubric that will be used to score your writing. Be sure to become familiar with the different categories. Notice that to score the highest (5–6), you must write an excellent piece that has a creative style, is free of grammar and spelling mistakes, and covers the topic thoroughly. Your writing must also flow smoothly while being logical. Make sure that each piece that you write has a definite beginning, middle, and end.

Note: A full explanation of the type of writing prompts and passages that will be on the 2009 assessment can be found at:

http://www.state.nj.us/education/

Language Arts Literacy
Writing
New Jersey Holistic Scoring Rubric - Grades 6 and 7

In scoring, consider the grid of written language	Inadequate Command	Limited Command	Partial Command	Adequate Command	Strong Command	Superior Command
Score	1	2	3	4	5	6
Content & Organization	*May lack opening and/or closing *Minimal response to topic; uncertain focus *No planning evident; disorganized *Details random, inappropriate, or barely apparent	*May lack opening and/or closing *Attempts to focus *May drift or shift focus *Attempts organization *Few, if any, transitions between ideas *Details lack elaboration that could highlight paper	*May lack opening and/or closing *Usually has single focus *Some lapses or flaws in organization *May lack some transitions between ideas *Repetitious details *Several unelaborated details	*Generally has opening and/or closing *Single focus *Ideas loosely connected *Transition evident *Uneven development of details	*Opening and closing *Single focus *Sense of unity and coherence *Key ideas developed *Logical progression of ideas *Moderately fluent *Attempts compositional risks *Details appropriate and varied	*Opening and closing *Single, distinct focus *Unified and coherent *Well-developed *Logical progression of ideas *Fluent, cohesive *Compositional risks successful *Details effective, vivid, explicit, and/or pertinent
Usage	*No apparent control *Severe/numerous errors	*Numerous errors	*Errors/patterns of errors may be evident	*Some errors that do not interfere with meaning	*Few errors	*Very few, if any, errors
Sentence Construction	*Assortment of incomplete and/or incorrect sentences	*Excessive monotony/same structure *Numerous errors	*Little variety in syntax *Some errors	*Some errors that do not interfere with meaning	*Few errors	*Very few, if any, errors
Mechanics	*Errors so severe they detract from meaning	*Numerous serious errors	*Patterns of errors evident	*No consistent pattern of errors *Some errors that do not interfere with meaning	*Few errors	*Very few, if any, errors
Nonscorable Responses	NR = No Response		Student wrote too little to allow reliable judgment of his/her writing.			

Nonscorable Responses		
NR = No Response	Student wrote too little to allow reliable judgment of his/her writing.	
OT = Off Topic/Off Task	Student did not write on the assigned topic/task, or the student attempted to copy the prompt.	
NE = Not English	Student wrote in a language other than English.	
WF = Wrong Format	Student refused to write on the topic, or the writing task folder was blank.	

Rubric Copyright New Jersey Department of Education; used with permission.

Chapter 1

WRITING A PERSUASIVE ESSAY—10 STEPS TO SUCCESS

MAJOR TASK: WRITE A PERSUASIVE ESSAY

The type of major essay writing you will do for the NJ ASK7 Language Arts Literacy Test is persuasive writing. Your essay needs to be five paragraphs long, well planned, and well written.

Prewriting is a strategy that you're probably using in your language arts class. The key is planning. To write effectively, every writer needs first to plan effectively. Good planning allows you, the writer, to collect your thoughts before you write them down on paper.

Let's do a brief exercise to get ready for the test. First, let's look at the writing prompt and then at the plans that two students have written before writing their own essays.

Strategic Practice

Write an essay that convinces your classmates to listen to either your favorite music or musical group. Make a writing plan for your essay before you begin writing.

In the space provided, write down the type of music you like best and list three main reasons for your choice. (See the Appendix, page 275, for additional graphic organizers that you may choose to use to organize your thoughts.)

My favorite type of music is _____ hip hop _____

I like this music because:

1. nice _____
2. cool rhythm _____
3. sounds cool _____

Now, check your answers as you read through Ronnie's and Billy's answers. See how your answers compare to theirs.

Ronnie's Plan

My favorite type of music is hip hop.

I like this music because:

1. It's awesome!
2. It really gives me a rush.
3. It's great to listen to.

The reasons that Ronnie gives don't show a lot of thought. Rather, Ronnie's response is emotional and needs to have some facts.

Good persuasive arguments use facts rather than emotions to convince the reader. Without good facts, these emotions can't support an opinion.

Let's look at Billy's plan next to see if his reasons are better ones.

Billy's Plan

My favorite type of music is hip hop.

I like this music because:

1. It has danceable "street" rhythms.
2. It speaks to the soul of young urban listeners.
3. It deals with important issues for my generation.

As you can see, Billy's plan is the better one. The reasons that are given can be supported with facts, rather than emotions.

Writing a Persuasive Essay—10 Steps to Success

Check your list again. Did you

- choose a specific type of music as your favorite?
- give three good reasons for your choice?

Warm-up Exercise—Supporting Details

Okay, now write three supporting details for each of your main points. Be sure to give clear, specific reasons.

My favorite type of music is ___electronic___

I like this music because:

1. ___It moves me___
   a. ___When I listen to it I___
   b. _____
   c. _____

2. ___Cool rythm___
   a. ___the b___
   b. ___th___
   c. _____

3. ___It's cool___
   a. ___the ___ and the beats combined___
   b. _____
   c. _____

As you have just seen, each of your main points can be supported with more details. Let's look at one of the ways that Billy's pre-writing list can be expanded.

My favorite type of music is hip hop.

I like this music because:

1. It has danceable "street" rhythms.
    a. The beats are easy to follow.
    b. The dancing is freestyle and energetic.
    c. The dance style is unique (one-of-a-kind).

2. It speaks to the soul of young urban listeners.
    a. It understands problems with parents and other generations.
    b. It lets us have music that is different from adults' music.
    c. It gives us energy when we're tired or depressed.

3. It deals with important issues for my generation.
    a. It mentions mistrust and anger.
    b. It mentions poverty and crime.
    c. It mentions misfits and rebels.

Billy's plan should be more successful than Ronnie's plan. You see, Billy's thesis (main point) is: "Hip Hop—My Favorite Music." The three reasons are clear and distinct. They're not just restatements of reasons already given. Finally, the supporting details help to explain each position.

   Billy is heading for success because good planning leads to success. Ronnie, however, needs to do more work to focus on reasons, rather than emotions. Even though Ronnie feels connected with hip hop music, the reader won't feel the same connection unless Ronnie states each point clearly the way Billy has done.

Ronnie's Plan—Can It Be Better?

Ronnie actually can make a better plan. It's good to love hip hop music. Ronnie just needs to do a few simple things to write effectively.

1. Think of the first statement: "I like my music (hip hop) because it's awesome!" Next, ask the question "Why?"
    - We know that Ronnie enjoys listening to hip hop. Now Ronnie needs to identify what's "awesome" about hip hop.
        a. Does the beat make it "awesome"?
        b. Is it easy to dance to?
        c. Is it different than the other music that's being played and recorded?

2. Think of the second statement: "It (hip hop) really gives me a rush." Again, ask the question "Why?"
   - Maybe Ronnie likes the fact that the music deals with problems like those he faces at school or at home.
   - Maybe it's not like the music that adults listen to.
   - Hip hop may even let Ronnie get away from some problems and "get lost" in the words and the beat.

3. Think of the third statement: "It's (hip hop's) great to listen to!" Ronnie can identify the reasons why hip hop is "great to listen to."
   - Maybe Ronnie has a problem (trouble with a friend who can't be trusted, for example) that is also in a song by a favorite singer or group.
   - Maybe Ronnie understands the anger in the music because of his own lack of money or a safe place to live.
   - Maybe both Ronnie and the musicians don't see much hope for the future.

Whatever the case may be, Ronnie's essay can be a good one if it includes some hard facts that give reasons for the feelings that have been written down.

PRE-WRITING YOUR WAY TO SUCCESS

Let's take a look at the first five steps of the Ten-Step Strategic Plan for Success. We'll practice these together. They are the Prewriting Steps. They'll help to make your writing clear and complete. Like Billy, you'll create a plan that's thoughtful, carefully put together, and headed toward success. With practice, you'll get better at coming up with the most important information for your essay. You'll be starting your writing with a solid plan.

BEFORE THE TEST BEGINS—FOCUS AND PREPARE TO WRITE

This step may be taken for granted, but it's critical in your effort to succeed. Unless you're giving it all of your attention, your chances for success will begin to drop. To be successful, you need to

- give your full attention to writing an effective persuasive essay.
- relax, take a deep breath or two, and get ready to do your best.

Remember, you need to be ready right from the start for this challenging test. There is not a lot of time for warming up.

Please note:

- When you take the test, remember to leave yourself enough time to write and edit your work.
- Write the response that you are being asked to write. If the directions say to write an essay, you should write an essay. On the other hand, you should write a letter if you are being asked to do so. Also, don't write a poem when you are being asked to write an essay or a letter.
- Remember, a good essay or letter is specific. Your writing must also be specific.

TEN-STEP STRATEGIC PLAN FOR SUCCESS

Let's look at the sample prompt. We'll go through each of the first five Prewriting Steps together. After each Step, a **Suggested Answer** is given. Compare each answer with the one that you've given.

STEP 1—READ THE PROMPT AND DIRECTIONS

This step is very important because it'll help you to start off well. Be sure to find out exactly what your topic is. This will help you to write directly for the prompt and address the questions that you've been given. Even if your essay is technically perfect, you'll receive a lower score if you didn't follow the prompt and all the necessary directions. Also, be sure to state your position clearly and concisely. Otherwise, you won't earn the high score you are looking to earn.

Writing Prompt

As a seventh grade student, you probably lead an active life. You go to school every day, do your homework after school, and then spend time doing things like playing sports, taking music lessons, "surfing" the Internet, or playing video games.

Because you don't always have a lot of time each day to do the things you like to do, you and other seventh graders often skip breakfast, lunch, and even dinner. Instead, you may often eat an unhealthy snack. This type of eating can lead to many health problems, including obesity, high blood pressure, and diabetes.

Moreover, these poor eating habits could actually hurt your ability to focus clearly on your lessons in classes. Your school, therefore, wants to eliminate all unhealthy meals at school and serve only healthy food and snacks in the cafeteria and in all vending machines.

Directions

Write an essay about your school's new policy to eliminate unhealthy foods and drinks from cafeteria meals and vending machines. Do you think this is a good policy? Do you think these changes will help you and your fellow students to be healthier? Do you believe that a policy like this one can actually change the eating habits of you and your friends? When you state your opinion, be specific. Make sure that you give enough supporting evidence for your argument. You may wish to include valid facts and examples, as well as brief anecdotes (very short personal stories) to prove your point.

Be sure to include your thesis (main point) in your opening paragraph.

Strategic Practice

Answer the following questions concerning the **Writing Prompt** and the **Directions** for the sample essay. After you answer these three questions, check your answers against those provided after this mini-quiz.

1. The practice of seventh-grade students skipping meals may lead to _____

   A. obesity

   B. high blood pressure

   C. diabetes

   D. all of the above

2. The new policy mentioned in the **Directions** would _____

   A. eliminate unhealthy foods and drinks from your school's cafeteria meals and vending machines.

   B. eliminate unhealthy meals and drinks from your school's vending machines.

   C. eliminate certain unhealthy foods and drinks from your school's vending machines.

   D. begin a study to determine whether unhealthy foods and drinks should be eliminated from your school's cafeteria meals and vending machines.

3. You, the essay writer must _____

   A. use a set of facts provided for the essay.

   B. state your opinion specifically.

   C. use facts to support your argument.

   D. do both "B" (state your opinion specifically) and "C" (use facts to support your argument).

The Answers

1. The practice of seventh-grade students skipping meals may lead to: "D" (all of the above). Look at the first two sentences of the second paragraph. These clearly state that the poor eating habits of many seventh graders "*can lead to many health problems, including obesity, high blood pressure, and diabetes.*"

2. The new policy mentioned in the **Directions** would: "A" (eliminate unhealthy foods and drinks from the school's cafeteria meals and vending machines). This answer is found in the first sentence of the **Directions** section: "*Write an essay about your school's new policy to eliminate unhealthy foods and drinks from cafeteria meals and vending machines.*" This is the statement that you will use to create your main idea (or thesis). This is the basis of your entire essay. Answer "B" doesn't mention "your school's cafeteria meals," and answer "C" is incorrect because of the word "certain." (By the way, answer "D" ["*Begin a study to determine …*"] is never mentioned in the **Directions** and is therefore incorrect.)

3. You, the essay writer, must: "D" (both "B" and "C," *state your opinion specifically* and *use facts to support your argument*). This answer can be found in the fifth and sixth sentences of the **Directions** section: "*When you state your opinion, be specific.*

Make sure that you give enough supporting evidence for your argument."

HOW AM I DOING? SHOULD I MOVE AHEAD OR PRACTICE?

How did you do with these questions? Were they easy for you to answer, or were they difficult? **If you did well** on this section, then **skip** to **Step 2—Working Title**.

If you struggled with this section, however, then you may be having trouble remembering the main points being covered. **Try practicing** by skimming over the material quickly and jotting down the key words that you find. Either practice this technique on a separate sheet of paper or simply highlight the key words in the **Writing Prompt** and **Directions**.

Now that you've finished, compare your list with the following one.

- seventh-grade students
- active lives
- skip meals . . . for unhealthy snack
- health problems
- new policy
- eliminate unhealthy foods

Once this practice exercise is completed, return to the **Writing Prompt** and the **Directions**. Re-read them carefully. This strategy should help you to improve your comprehension.

Now move on to **Step 2—Working Title**.

STEP 2—WORKING TITLE

Steps 2 and 3 are "organizing" steps that will help you create a "map" for your writing. First begin by thinking of a **Working Title**. Next, list your thesis (main idea). You may wish to use a graphic organizer (flow chart, ideas web, or writing wheel), a formal outline, or a series of notes for each paragraph. For this exercise, a graphic organizer will be used with boxes containing bullet points.

Do I Really Need to Start with a Title Now?

An author will often change the title of an essay before settling on the final one. It's good practice, however, to begin writing with a working title in place. This working title gives direction to your essay. It can be a guide to tell you whether your thoughts are staying on topic or wandering from your original direction.

When deciding on a working title, always keep in mind the position that you're taking. Your title must directly reflect your stance. Otherwise, the first impression you make on the evaluators of your test will not be positive. At the start, your title and your thesis (main point) will look a lot like each other.

Strategic Practice

Here's Your Task: Create your own effective writing plan. Take a clear, specific position for this task: "Write an essay about the new policy that would eliminate unhealthy foods and drinks from your school's cafeteria meals and vending machines at school." Your main idea will be your position on this statement: Do you support or oppose the position? For this exercise, we will take the position that "unhealthy foods and drinks should be eliminated from your school's cafeteria meals and vending machines."

Let's examine the following sample titles and decide which ones we may or may not use for this essay.

1. *Kids Should Eat Healthy Foods*
   This title makes good sense with its message. Even so, it does not directly address the main question.
2. *Parents Need to Feed Their Kids Better Meals*
   This title is a supporting detail and is therefore not strong enough to stand alone as a main point.
3. *We Need Healthier Food and Drink Choices in My School*
   This title does address the main question, and it is a good one.
4. *Kids at My School Eat Too Much Junk*
   This title is a supporting detail that is a bit too general: we don't know how much junk food and drinks are actually too much.
5. *My School Should Stop Selling Junk Food and Drinks*
   This title does address the main question and may be a possibility.

6. *A Junk Food Ban at My School*
   This title would be a good one if it also included drink choices.

At this point, the graphic organizer that we're using would look this way.

> **Working Title**
>
> We Need Healthier Food and Drink Choices in My School

STEP 3—THESIS STATEMENT (MAIN IDEA)

Now that you have your **Working Title**, you need to write a clear **Thesis Statement (Main Idea)**. Remember, your thesis is just a restatement of your **Working Title**.

Strategic Practice

The **Working Title** is "We Need Healthier Food and Drink Choices in My School." Place a checkmark in the blank before the **Thesis Statement (Main Idea)** that you feel is the best one for this essay.

1. ____ Unhealthy foods should be banned from schools.

2. __✓_ Unhealthy drinks should be banned from my school.

3. ____ Unhealthy foods and drinks should be eliminated in my school.

4. ____ We should be allowed to eat anything we want in school.

The Answers

1. The statement "Unhealthy foods should be banned from schools" does not include either unhealthy drinks or the term "my school," which are mentioned in the **Working Title**.
2. The statement "Unhealthy drinks should be banned from my school" does not include unhealthy foods, which are mentioned in the **Working Title**.

3. The statement "Unhealthy foods and drinks should be eliminated in my school" is the best one because it includes all the important information from the **Working Title**.
4. The statement "We should be allowed to eat anything we want in school" is the opposite of the information presented in the **Working Title**.

Now, fill in the graphic organizer with the **Working Title** and **Answer #3** from the exercise you have just completed.

Working Title

We Need Healthier Food and Drink Choices in My School

↓

- **Thesis Statement (Main Idea)**
  - Unhealthy foods and drinks should be eliminated in my school.

STEP 4—MAKE A "COMMON SENSE" CHECK

Before continuing with the next step, consider these questions:

- Does my **Thesis Statement (Main Idea)** make sense?
- Am I stating my thesis clearly?
- Am I saying what I want to say?
- Does my idea make sense?

A "common sense" check is a good strategy to use when practicing for the NJ ASK Test. This strategy will also help you when you are actually taking the test.

STEP 5—MAIN POINTS AND SUPPORTING DETAILS

Before writing the essay, let's continue getting organized. This step helps you to make a clear "map" to follow as you compose your thoughts. You should be able to stay on topic easier. Also, you should reduce your chances of forgetting a main point in your essay.

Main Points—Identification

Let's identify our three main points. Your first and third arguments should be your two strongest ones. Your first argument gives the test reviewer a strong first impression of your essay. In addition, putting your strongest argument third is a good strategy since it's the one the test reviewers will remember the most. Why? It's the last one they'll see. The last point being made is usually the first one being remembered.

Strategic Practice

Here's Your Task: Let's check these possible main points to see which ones are acceptable, then let's see which are the best. Remember, the main point of each paragraph needs to connect with the main idea (or thesis) of your essay.

1. *Kids today are eating too much.*
   This statement may or may not be true. What is important is this statement does not strongly support the thesis ("Unhealthy meals and drinks should be eliminated in my school").

2. *Parents need to feed their kids better meals.*
   This statement is not strong enough to be the first main point of this essay. Rather, it is possibly a supporting detail.

3. *We concentrate better when we're healthy.*
   Students who concentrate on their lessons usually do well in school. This point is a good one to use in your essay.

4. *Kids at my school eat too much junk food.*
   Even though both **school** and **junk food** are mentioned, you may wish to use it as a supporting detail instead of a main point.

5. *Our bodies are still growing so we need healthy food.*
   This is a reason based on medical fact. Good nutrition is important not just for seventh graders, but also for everyone. This is another good point to make in your essay.

6. *Consuming only healthy foods and drinks helps our families to take good care of us.*
   Parents are responsible for their children's health and welfare. Your school can help parents by serving healthy foods and drinks. This is a good point for your essay.

After completing this exercise, we can agree that we have found three main points. Since you only will have a total of 45 minutes to complete the essay writing section of the NJ ASK Language Arts Literacy Test for Grade 7, it is wise to use only three points to develop your essay. Otherwise, you may not have time to finish your essay and that will hurt your score a lot.

Let's look at our plan so far. We have four paragraphs. You'll write the final one (Paragraph 5). You see, it will have your summary and any little bit of extra thought you can add.

Fill in the Blanks

Take a look at the **Thesis (Main Idea)** and Paragraphs 2–4. Next, see if you can fill in the blanks with the **Supporting Details** for the Main Points in Paragraphs 2, 3, and 4.

- **Paragraph 1—Thesis (Main Idea)**
  - *Unhealthy foods and drinks should be eliminated in my school.*
    - *We concentrate better when we're healthy.*
    - *Having only healthy foods and drinks in our school helps our families to take good care of us.*
    - *Our bodies are still growing. That's the reason why we need healthy foods and drinks.*

- **Paragraph 2—First Main Point:** *We concentrate better when we're healthy.*

  (Hints: How will being able to concentrate better help you in school? What are the benefits of better concentration?)

  - *Supporting Detail #1* _Makes it to the child grades_
  - *Supporting Detail #2* _child won't be love the influence_
  - *Supporting Detail #3* _could stay hav mental issue_

- **Paragraph 3—Second Main Point:** *Having only healthy foods and drinks in our school helps our families to take good care of us.* (Hints: Do you and your family have time to make healthy meals at home? Does your schedule cause you to eat "on the run"? Why is that a problem?)

- *Supporting Detail #1* _____

- *Supporting Detail #2* _____

- *Supporting Detail #3* _____

■ Paragraph 4—Third Main Point: *Our bodies are still growing. That's the reason why we need healthy foods and drinks.* (Hints: What is the problem with fatty foods and sweet drinks? What are the benefits of avoiding them?)

- *Supporting Detail #1* _____

- *Supporting Detail #2* _____

- *Supporting Detail #3* _____

Check Out the Sample Answers

Now that you have filled in the blanks, take a look at the sample plan contained in the graphic organizer. Are your ideas similar to those in the organizer? If your plan is a better one, congratulations! If you struggled with this exercise, then carefully look over the sample plan and see if there is anything that could be added to your information.

Working Title

We Need Better Food and Drink Choices in My School

- **Main Idea (Thesis Statement)**
  - Eliminating unhealthy meals and snacks in my school is a good idea.

- **Main Point #1**—We concentrate better when we're healthy.
  - **Supporting Details**
    - We can pay attention better.
    - We can ask better questions and get better test scores.
    - We can learn more.

- **Main Point #2**—Eating only healthy foods and drinks helps our families to take good care of us.
  - **Supporting Details**
    - Many of us students from homes with working parents don't have someone to make us nutritional meals.
    - Many of us follow busy schedules that interfere with our good eating habits.
    - Making good nutrition choices can help us to stay healthy.

- **Main Point #3**—Our growing bodies need healthy food.
  - **Supporting Details**
    - We should avoid salty, fatty, sugary foods and caffeinated, sugary drinks.
    - Healthy foods and drinks can help us students to fight off diseases, colds, and flu.
    - Making these healthy choices can help us to stay healthy.

Summary Conclusion
- Restate the Thesis (Main Idea).
- Restate the Three Main Points.
- Add the Final Conclusion.

STEP 6—SUMMARY CONCLUSION

Now that you have completed the exercise dealing with **Main Points and Supporting Details**, you need to restate your **Thesis Statement (Main Idea)** and each of your **Main Points** clearly in your **Summary Conclusion**.

Strategic Practice

So far, you have practiced with the first four paragraphs of your essay. These may be the hardest to write. Once you get to the fifth paragraph, you'll restate your thesis (main idea). Next, you'll summarize (highlight) the main point you have made in each paragraph. You'll then draw a final conclusion from the points you have made.

It's Time to Close

Now, write a sample closing paragraph. Use either the supporting details that you made in the previous exercise or use the information in the sample graphic organizer.

_____

_____

_____

_____

_____

_____

_____

Now that you are finished writing, compare your **Summary Conclusion** with the following one. As you do, ask yourself: Did I remember to

- begin with my **Thesis Statement (Main Idea)**?
- restate each of my **Main Points**?
- make a thoughtful closing statement?

Sample Summary Conclusion

Healthier foods and drinks in my school could give us students a better chance to be healthy each day. We can concentrate better when we are healthy. Our families can benefit because we will be making better nutritional choices. Our growing bodies need healthy food so our bodies can be in good physical shape. By making these good nutritional choices, we are developing good habits that will benefit us for the rest of our lives.

Helpful Hint

When you're writing your essay, there's a chance you won't know your final conclusion until you reach the end of the essay. **Don't panic!** You can still do well by writing a solid essay. Often, your final conclusion will seem to appear magically as you're finishing your essay. The key is to remain calm.

STEP 7—USE TRANSITIONS

Transitional phrases are a critical element to help you to succeed on the NJ ASK Language Arts Literacy Test for Grade 7. They indicate many things including **time** ("Immediately" or "Then"), **sequence** ("First of all" or "At this point"), **comparison** ("However" or "Nonetheless"), or **summary** ("Therefore" or "As a result").

Strategic Practice

Let's examine the following statements to practice using transitional phrases. For each sentence, choose the correct transitional word or phrase to fill in the blank.

1. If we consume healthier foods and drinks in school, _____ we have a better chance to concentrate better.

    A. next

    B. when

    C. then

    D. therefore

2. Our growing bodies need healthy food. _____, we should eat a healthy diet both at home and at school.

    A. Therefore

    B. In contrast

    C. Also

    D. First of all

3. We should avoid salty snacks. _____, we should avoid sugary snacks and drinks.

    A. Therefore

    B. In contrast

    C. Also

    D. Finally

The Answers

1. **A.** The word *next* doesn't work well here since consuming *healthier food and drinks in school* should result in *a better chance* for the students to *concentrate better*. The word next would work better if this sentence were describing steps in a sequence: *First of all, Second,* and *Next.*
   B. The word *when* doesn't work. It creates a sentence fragment.
   C. The word *then* is the correct choice. The phrase *If . . . then* uses correct grammar and connects the two main parts of the sentence.
   D. Even though the word *therefore* introduces a conclusion, it is nonetheless not the proper choice. Should the word *If* be omitted at the beginning of the sentence, then the use of the word *therefore* would be acceptable to begin the second sentence.

2. **A.** The word *Therefore* is used correctly because it shows that eating *a healthy diet both at home and at school* is an appropriate choice because *our growing bodies need healthy food*. The second statement directly supports the first.
   B. The phrase *In contrast* is incorrect in this sentence since the second statement is the result of the first. There is no *contrast*.
   C. The word *Also* is not the best choice here since the two sentences are connected. *Also* is better used for additional information that is not necessarily related directly to the first sentence.
   D. *First of all* is not a good choice unless it is part of a larger paragraph. It needs to introduce this point as the first of one or more additional points.

3. **A.** *Therefore* is not a good choice since the second statement *(avoid sugary snacks and drinks)* is an additional statement to support the first one *(avoid salty snacks)*.
   B. *In contrast* is not a good choice. The two sentences are closely related but not opposites.
   C. *Also* is the correct choice since it shows that the second sentence is being added to the first. Use *Also* in a similar way to your use of a plus sign (+) in math class.
   D. *Finally* is not a good choice since there is only one sentence coming before the second and final sentence. The word *Finally* should be used only in a series of three or more sentences or ideas.

STEP 8—BEGIN WITH A "GRABBER"

All successful persuasive essays raise the readers' interest or get their attention through the use of grabbers. These are often used by public speakers to capture the audience's attention quickly. You can do the same for the evaluators of your essay.

An effective **"Grabber"** should make the reader want to learn more about the subject you're covering in your essay. The grabber should always relate directly to the topic of the essay, even when it is shocking. Otherwise, the effect is similar to your hearing a door slam while you're watching a tense moment in a movie, a drama, or a sporting event on TV. The noise shocks you, but it has no relation to what you're watching. You may quickly look around to find out where the noise is coming from, but then you turn your attention back to your TV set. An effective grabber therefore should not be similar to the sound of a slamming door. Rather, it should be similar to a pleasant invitation, a welcoming handshake, or a meaningful shock.

When you write your essay, try one of the following devices.

Sample Grabbers

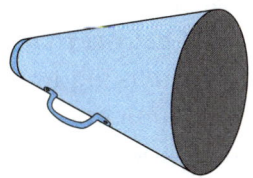

1. Rhetorical Question

A **rhetorical question** is one that you do not expect to be answered. It is asked to get your readers to wonder about an issue. You, the writer will supply the appropriate answer.

Here are some examples.

- Have you ever considered . . . ?
- What pops into your mind when you hear the word . . . ?
- When you are invited to a friend's birthday party, do you ever think about . . . ?

2. Interesting Fact or Observation

An **interesting fact or observation** leads the reader to become interested in your essay. When you relate this information, you expect your reader to smile, to nod in agreement, or to feel that (s)he has just learned something important.

Here are some examples.

- Margarine has one less molecule than plastic.
- The first Harley-Davidson motorcycle used a tomato can for a carburetor (old-fashioned fuel regulator on a car's engine).
- Your body has ten times more bacteria cells than human cells.
- There are over 100 million Web sites on the Internet.

3. Startling Statement

Use a **startling statement** to shock or get an emotional reaction from your reader. Use statements that are thought to be common knowledge because you can't look them up during the test.

- Excessive cell phone use may expose you to harmful radiation.
- Secondhand smoke kills many innocent victims each year.
- Drug abuse is found not only in poor communities, but also in rich ones.

> **Helpful Hint**
>
> Often, it is easier to write your "Grabber" after you have compiled all your information. In this way, you will have a better chance that your "Grabber" will fit your essay.

Strategic Practice

Sometimes the hardest part of writing an essay is writing the opening line. With a good opening line, your essay will get off to a great start. The idea is to grab the reader's attention by making her or him interested in hearing the main points of your argument. For example, for an essay about replacing grades at your school with a "Pass/Fail" system, you might write: "Learning a skill or different information should be important because it is helpful, not because it leads to a grade in school."

Let's practice by writing some opening first lines for the topics listed.

Topic #1—Students should not be allowed to use computers in your school.

_____

_____

_____

Topic #2—There should be Saturday detention in your school.

_____

_____

_____

Topic #3—Your school should extend the day one hour so you and your fellow students can complete your homework.

_____

_____

_____

STEP 9—WRITING

This is the step to use to create your persuasive essay. When you actually take the test, allow yourself enough time to write your essay. Try to take no more than ten minutes of planning before you begin writing. With practice, you might even reduce your pre-writing time to five minutes or so.

Strategic Practice

Here are some strategies to use as you practice your essay writing for the test.

- Once you've completed your pre-writing and before you begin your essay, look at the clock to see how much of the original 45 minutes remain.
- After you complete your first two paragraphs, glance at the clock to see how much time you now have left.
  - If you have plenty of time, don't rush but don't slow down either. Instead, be sure to maintain your steady pace.
  - If you lag behind a bit, then you'll need to increase your pace.
  - It is important that you finish your essay since your score will be lowered for a partial essay.
- After you finish writing your essay, look at your title again.
  - If it fits your essay, then keep it.
  - If the title doesn't fit, then change it.
- When you write your essay, be sure to use words that you know are used correctly and spelled correctly.

Helpful Hint

If you're not sure of either the meaning or the proper spelling of a word, then use a different word that you **are** sure of. Correct spelling and good word choice do make a difference in your score.

STEP 10—PROOFREAD AND EDIT

This is the final step in writing your essay. Once you've finished writing, take a deep breath. This will only take a few seconds, but it should relax you enough to get you ready to proofread and edit your essay. Carefully read over your essay. You should only need to add a finishing touch or two.

It is important for you to plan carefully **before** you begin to write your final draft. In this way, you can avoid any major rewrites that will take up too much time.

To make sure that your essay receives the best score, you must proofread and edit your final draft. Remember, the content and the development of your essay are important. Also, don't forget that spelling, punctuation, and grammar count, too.

Writing Checklist for NJ ASK

As you read over your essay, be sure that you use the NJ ASK Writer's Checklist. This is available on the NJ PEP Web site at www.njpep.org . This site is sponsored by the New Jersey Department of Education. Just go to the Web site and type "NJ ASK Writer's Checklist" in the "Search" box.

Here is a brief version of the NJ ASK Writer's Checklist. It covers all the major points in the actual NJ ASK Writer's Checklist. Use either checklist to evaluate the four major areas of your writing.

√ Have I started with an overview paragraph that contains my main point (thesis)?
√ Does my formal persuasive essay make sense?
√ Is my position clear?
√ Have I given details, explanations, and examples to support each of my three main points?
√ Am I bringing my essay to a logical conclusion by restating my main points?
√ Are my sentences clear and varied?
√ Are my words vivid and powerful?
√ Have I used my words correctly?
√ Is my capitalization, spelling, and punctuation correct?
√ Have I written neatly so the test evaluators can read what I'm saying?

Strategic Practice

Let's practice with the following essay draft that a student like you might write. As you edit the essay, look for spelling mistakes, grammar mistakes, and logic errors. Mark up all the mistakes you find.

When you have completed editing the essay, check your answers with those from the sample. You might find some helpful editing suggestions.

WE NEED BETTER FOOD AND DRINK CHOICES IN MY SCHOOL

If our school gave grades for the meals and drinks that many of us are eating and drinking in school, would we get a lot of failing grades? Many of us students aren't eating healthy lunches and snacks. These poor choices are harmful ones. Our general health and concentration is being affected. And our families can't always provide us with the right nutritional choices. So, we should eliminate the serving of unhealthy meals and snacks in our school.

By making better nutritional choices, we can increase our chances of focusing more directly on our lessons. Sugar and caffeine, which are common ingredients in many snack foods and drinks, have a bad affect on our ability to maintain our concentration. We can pay attention in class and ask more thoughtful questions when we are not being distracted by the "rush" and the "slump" we get from these snacks. When we learn more, we can have a better chance to get higher scores on our quizzes, tests, and projects.

Eliminating unhealthy meals and snacks in school will help our bodies to develop more properly. We should avoid foods and snacks that are not only high in sugar and caffeine, but in fats and salt. We need to stay strong to fight off and prevent various diseases like the common cold and the flew. We should try to stay healthy in our young years to avoid increasing our chances of becoming a victim of various diseases including high blood pressure, diabetes, bone diseases, and heart problems. The habits we establish now most likely will be the ones we will follow when we get older.

By making healthy food choices, we can also help our parents or guardians. Many of us live in "single parent" homes and homes in which our parents or guardians both work. We also have very busy schedules that we follow each day as we go to school, do our chores, play on teams, practice our musical instruments, "surf" the internet, play video games, listen to music, and spend time with our friends. Many of our schedules don't match with those of our parents or guardians. That is why we need help to make the correct nutritional choices, and our school can actually help us by making sure that our food and snacks are healthy ones.

By not eating the right foods and snacks in school, we are potentially causing ourselves a great deal of harm. We are hurting ourselves in the classroom by affecting our ability not only to concentrate, but also to do our best work. We are hurting our bodies by weakening our defenses against everyday problems like colds *and flu and more severe problems including diabetes and heart disease. We are hurting our parents' or guardians' chances of helping us to be healthy since we are all following busy and hectic schedules that do not always allow us time to make the best food choices. We often choose the most convenient choices instead. I therefore believe that eliminating unhealthy meals and snacks in school is an idea that should be adopted today. Shouldn't we all try to receive a passing grade for our food choices as we grow up to be reasonable, intelligent, and healthy adults?*

(Please check page 235, Chapter 8, Answer Keys and Explanations, for a corrected sample of this essay. Be sure to read the reason given for each correction. Your answers may be different. Make sure that all your suggestions are both correct and fitting for the essay.)

INDEPENDENT WRITING PRACTICE

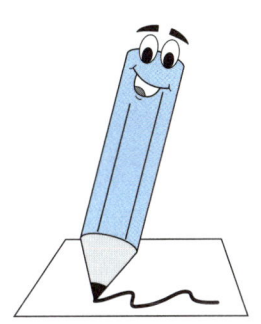

Now that you have followed the entire writing process from beginning to end, it's time to practice your persuasive writing skills by yourself. Use the space provided to pre-write. Organize your ideas in a flow chart, ideas web, outline with bullet points, or any reasonable way that works best for you.

When you finish, check the **Suggested Main Points** listed on page 237 in the **Answer Key**. Your points may be just as good, if not better than the ones given.

Topic #1

"Parents for Change," a local community group of concerned parents, is challenging the standard grading scale used in your school. They believe that under the present system, high grades are too easy to achieve. That is the reason they are calling for a stricter scale that would change the traditional ten-point scale ("100" to "90" is an "A," "89" to "80" is a "B," etc.) to a seven-point scale ("100" to "93" is an "A," "92" to "85" is a "B," etc.). Write a letter to this group and explain your opinion to them.

Pre-writing Section

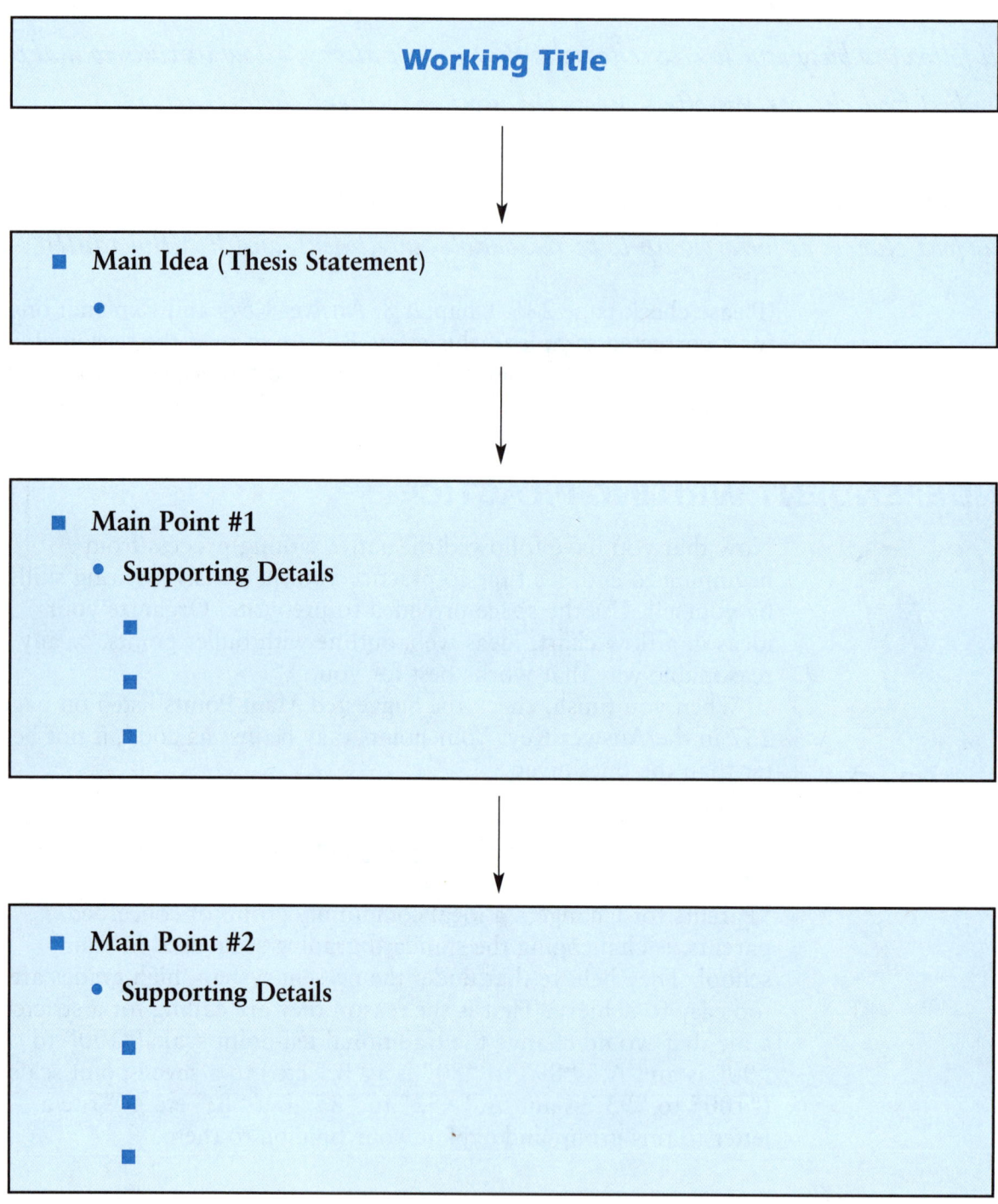

- Main Point #3
  - Supporting Details
    - ▪
    - ▪
    - ▪

Summary Conclusion
- Restate the Thesis (Main Idea).
- Restate the Three Main Points.
  - ▪
  - ▪
  - ▪
- Add the Final Conclusion.

Topic #1—Essay

Title: _____

_____

_____

_____

_____

Chapter 2

WRITING A SPECULATIVE ESSAY—10 STEPS TO SUCCESS

SOME KEY QUESTIONS

What is the new section that has been added to the NJ ASK7 Language Arts Literacy Test?

It is the Speculative Writing Test. You will write a story using only a few details given in the test directions. The story is a 25-minute exercise that was graded as a draft in 2008. These conditions are likely to change in the future.

What skills do I need to have to get a good score on this test?

You will need to have a good imagination. When you speculate, you use your imagination. You will need to have a good idea for your story and tell the complete story. You will need to write your story around a conflict that you will resolve. You will need to give enough details so your reader understands your story. You will need to bring your story to a logical conclusion. Finally, you will need to use correct grammar and spelling.

What will I have to write about?

You will be given a brief description of a situation. Then, you will be asked to think about what you feel might happen as the situation develops. In other words, you'll be asked to write a story from the details you're given. For example, if you're given a situation in which a youngster has wandered too far from home, you might be asked to tell the story of the things that happen next.

What should I include in my story?

You should write your story so your reader knows exactly what is happening. Make sure that your story makes sense. Write your story to answer the question you're being asked. In other words, don't write about an adventure in an amusement park if your question deals with a lost child trying to return home.

Should I pre-write (make notes to plan my writing) before I actually begin?

You should always pre-write before you begin writing. By doing so, you will organize your thoughts, create your plan for writing, and actually warm up your brain to prepare yourself for a good writing session.

CREATING A STORY PLAN

Writing a story for the Speculative Writing portion of the New Jersey ASK Grade 7 Language Arts Test is different than writing a persuasive essay. In the first chapter of this book, you were concerned with taking a position and developing a thoughtful argument that was supported by three main points. That strategy won't work for this section.

To write an effective story, you need a new plan. For your persuasive essay, you practiced using mostly logic and reasoning to create an effective argument. For your speculative essay, you're going to use your imagination to "speculate" what might happen in a certain situation. You will not be arguing your point. Instead, you will be addressing the main question, "What do you think is happening?"

Time to Practice

Imagine that you have a Chihuahua puppy. Your Chihuahua puppy is a very excitable dog that always seems to have a lot of energy. Today, you hear your dog barking more loudly than usual. Think about what might be causing your dog to be so excited.

Once you decide upon the cause of your Chihuahua's barking, then create a story and fill in the details of that story. Remember, your story should be based on events that most people would understand.

Please remember that our practice throughout this book is meant to be completed at a slower pace than you will have when you take the actual test itself. By practicing in the book, you should be able to gain the skills needed to work **at a much faster pace**.

STEP #1—CREATE THE REALISTIC MAIN CONFLICT

The first thing we need to do is to think about possible situations (story lines or plots) for this story. These will each be created from a main conflict (problem). For this exercise, we will use the following scenario: Your best friend hears the sounds of a puppy excitedly barking in the kitchen. For the conflict, let's imagine that the puppy smells smoke that is coming from the oven because the breakfast muffins are burning.

Second, think about the reason why the puppy might be discovering the beginning of a major problem. Consider not only the loss of one of the muffins for breakfast, but more importantly the safety hazard that might occur. In the space given below, write down both what you think the main conflict is and the reason why the muffins burning could be a problem.

Conflict and Reason

_____
_____
_____
_____
_____
_____
_____

A possible response may be that the muffins that are baking in the oven have started to smoke and will soon catch fire. The smoke from the fire has just started and hasn't yet reached the smoke detector. Even so, this fire is dangerous because your friend's mom is in the backyard and doesn't see that the muffins are starting to burn. Your friend has just awakened and is getting out of bed upstairs. The puppy has noticed the smoke, and it begins to bark while running back and forth in front of the stove. Meanwhile, if the muffins catch fire, then the entire kitchen might also catch fire. That would be terrible.

Consider now what the main conflict is. Is it

- your friend not realizing that the puppy's barking is really a warning of a possible fire in the house?
- the muffins smoking and being close to catching fire?

The main problem is the "possible fire in the house." Even so, this situation has become a problem because your friend does not realize that the muffins are starting to burn. Your friend being awakened when (s)he hears the puppy barking and scurrying around is a good starting point for the story.

STEP #2—CREATE THE PLOT (PLAN OF ACTION)

The next step to consider is creating the plot (plan of action) for the story. Here are some important questions that you can pose. Answer each question in the space provided.

- What is your friend thinking when (s)he hears the puppy barking?

_____

_____

_____

_____

- Is the puppy's behavior usual or not? If so, when are the other times that the puppy has barked? What makes your friend take notice when the puppy is barking this time?

  _____
  _____
  _____
  _____

- Is your friend a worrier? Does (s)he panic? Whatever the case may be, your friend's personality can easily be a major part of your story line.

  _____
  _____
  _____
  _____

- How badly are the muffins smoking? Has the smoke started to fill the room? How close are the muffins to catching fire?

  _____
  _____
  _____
  _____

STEP #3—CREATE THE SETTING

Think about the setting of your story. When you write your story for the test, be sure to include details. This makes your story seem real. Also, paint a thorough word picture to give your reader a clear view of your scenes.

As an exercise, write down one detail to describe your friend's room. If you practice this technique, you'll train your mind to begin to think of these details automatically. You won't have much time on the actual NJ ASK Test, so to improve your story you'll need to jot down maybe one detail. The amount of detail that you will be able to include and the length of your story will depend on the amount of time it takes you to write an effective story. Remember, this is a timed test. Once the time runs out, you cannot return to the test to finish an item.

- Detail

_____

_____

Next, do the same for your kitchen.

- Detail

_____

_____

Here is a possible detail for your friend's room.

- Detail—There is an old clock radio that wakes her up in the morning.

Here is a possible detail for your friend's kitchen.

- Detail—The window shade was blocking the sun from shining directly on the door leading into the kitchen.

STEP #4—GIVE EACH MAIN CHARACTER A PERSONALITY

Now it's time to jot down a brief outline of the facts of the story so far. Fill in the information next to each section.

Two (or More) Personality Traits and a Name for Each Main Character

- **Friend**
  - Trait #1
    _____

  - When does your friend show this trait?
    _____
    _____
    _____

  - Trait #2
    _____

  - When does your friend show this trait?
    _____
    _____
    _____

  - Name
    _____

- **Puppy**
  - Trait #1
    _____

  - When does the dog show this trait?
    _____
    _____
    _____

- Trait #2

  _____

- When does the dog show this trait?

  _____

  _____

  _____

- Name

  _____

Here is a sample of some possible responses.

■ Friend
- Name—JJ Wilburn
- Gender—Female
- Trait #1—Reliable
- When does your friend show this trait? She always helps out in an emergency. She fed the dog belonging to Mr. Barnes, a neighbor, every day until he returned from the hospital last summer.
- Trait #2—Quick to take action
- When does your friend show this trait? When another student was being bullied at school, your friend stepped in and told the others to stop. She didn't hesitate at all.

■ Dog
- Name—Frisky
- Gender—Male
- Trait #1—Full of Energy
- When does the dog show this trait? Like most puppies, this one seems to have an unlimited supply of energy. One day, the puppy ran around the house almost non-stop for ten minutes. One minute later, the puppy was gobbling down its food. Ten minutes later, the puppy was sleeping to rest up for the next dash around the house.
- Trait #2—Loyal
- When does the dog show this trait? The puppy appreciates the love he receives in the Wilburn house. JJ is always taking

him for walks and play sessions outside. Mrs. Wilburn lets the dog sit in her lap after JJ goes to sleep. While Mrs. Wilburn watches her favorite program, Frisky falls asleep too.

STEP #5—DEVELOP THE STORY (PLOT LINE)

The next step is to create a plot line. You may use the plot line as a plan for the action in your story. You will focus on "setting the stage," identifying the problem (conflict), creating the action (rising action), and then solving the problem (resolution).

Action

Think about the action taking place. After waking up and getting out of bed, your friend hears the new puppy barking and scurrying around the kitchen. Consider these questions as you prepare to write your story.

1. What does your friend think is the reason for the puppy barking and running around so much?

   _____

   _____

2. Does your friend investigate immediately the reason why the puppy is excited, or does (s)he wait a few moments? Why?

   _____

   _____

3. When the muffins catch fire, what happens next?

   _____

   _____

4. How does your friend deal with the fire? Was anything badly damaged?

   _____

   _____

5. What is the lesson that your friend and her or his mom learn from this experience?

_____

_____

Here are some possible responses to the questions that were just asked.

1. What does your friend think is the reason for the puppy barking and running around so much?

   Your friend might think that the puppy is just excited about one of his toys or maybe a bird that has flown by.

2. Does your friend investigate immediately the reason why the puppy is excited, or does (s)he wait a few moments? Why?

   Your friend might yawn, stretch a little, and then walk downstairs to try to find out the reason why the puppy is barking so much.

3. When the muffins were smoking and almost ready to catch fire, what happens next?

   Your friend might start to fill up a bucket with water to throw on the flames. However, (s)he might remember the previous conversation with Uncle Ralph, the firefighter, about throwing water on a fire. You friend may also realize that there may be an exposed electric wire, and water could also be dangerous in that situation. Therefore, before the fire gets too large to manage, your friend opens a box of salt and throws it on the fire to douse it.

STEP #6—WRITE THE SOLUTION FOR THE PROBLEM (RESOLVE THE CONFLICT)

This is the point where your story begins to wrap up. The events have developed, and the solution lies just ahead.

Here are some questions for you to consider for this step.

1. How does your friend deal with the fire? Was anything badly damaged?

   Luckily, your friend thought clearly and was able to put out the fire.

2. What is the lesson that your friend and her or his mom learn from this experience?

   The lesson might be, "When you are cooking or baking, don't ever leave the stove unattended."

STEP #7—GIVE YOUR STORY A WORKING TITLE

When you write a story, you must always give it a title. This title should relate to the events of your story. It should, in fact, reflect the main conflict in some way. Also, it should make the reader want to read your story because the title sounds exciting.

Which of these titles do you think fits your story the best?

1. My New Puppy
2. My Friend JJ's Noisy Puppy
3. My Friend Hates to Wake Up

The first title "My New Puppy" would be better for a story about getting a new puppy. The second title is a better one because it relates somewhat to the action of the story. The third one isn't good because it sounds like the story deals with your friend's dislike for waking up.

Even though the second title is not a great one, it's the best one of the bunch. Let's use it for now until you actually write the story. Once you're done, the title may be easier to write.

Using the information that you have gathered from our guided pre-write, please write a draft of your speculative story. Be sure to get all your ideas down on paper before you even begin to think about editing. Make sure that you do the following as you write:

- Start with a realistic situation.
  - Consider writing about things you know.
  - Keep your ideas realistic, or at least clear and precise.
- Introduce your main conflict. Tell about:
  - The problem that seems to be happening.
  - The reason that the situation being described is a problem.

- Pay attention to the plot of your story.
  - Write your story so it relates directly to your plot.
  - Be sure that your story makes sense so the adults who will be scoring your test can understand it.
- Give each of your characters a personality. Let your reader get close to your characters by:
  - Describing the way they look.
  - Showing their traits.
- Create the setting.
  - "Painting a word picture" that describes the characters and places in the scene.
  - Make sure that your scene "fits" your story and is not "out of place" or confusing.
- Develop the plot.
  - Write your story so the events follow a regular pattern.
  - Make sure that the events relate directly to your main conflict.
- Decide what the resolution will be.
  - Heroic action.
  - Unlikely happening.
- Give your story a working title. You may change it after the story is written. For now, however, it will give your story a point that you can focus upon.
- Consider whether or not a lesson was learned by the main character(s).
  - If so, does the lesson make sense from the story you have written?
  - If not, does the story come to a definite conclusion?

STEP #8—WRITE YOUR FIRST DRAFT

Speculative Story—Draft

Title _____

_____

_____

_____

_____

Here's a possible essay draft.

Title—My Friend JJ's Noisy Puppy

As the sun came up, JJ heard her alarm clock go off. She was asleep when some noise woke her up. The noise was from downstairs, and it was loud. She figured her mom would take care of business, but she didn't. How much louder could the noise become?

JJ always helped people. She stopped some bullies at school one time. She took care of a neighbor's dog.

As she walks out of her room, she was able to tell that the noise was being made by Frisky. Frisky sounded excited, but JJ figured that her puppy was acting the way it always did. This puppy would run around for almost ten minutes at a time. The barking was probably just Frisky's way of being psyched.

When JJ got downstairs, however, she noticed that something was berning. JJ called to her mom to ask if nothing was wrong, but her mom didn't answer. JJ called again, but she still didn't get an answer.

As JJ opened the door to the kitchen, the sun that would usually be in JJ's eyes was blocked since her mom had pulled down the shade. At once, JJ noticed that Frisky was barking and running around in circles. Before she tried to calm down her puppy, JJ noticed smoke. JJ had to act quick.

She started to fill up a bucket with water, but JJ remembered a conversation last week with her Uncle Ralph. JJ asked him if you throw water on a fire. He told her to do so if the fire isn't a grease or electrical fire. For those, he said to open a box of salt and throw the salt on the fire.

JJ was able to take as box of salt in case she needed to use it to put out the fire, make sure the fire hadn't started, open the door, and take out the muffins. JJ's mom raced into the kitchen.

JJ's mom asked her what had happened. JJ told her that Frisky woke her up, and she came down to turn off the oven. JJ thought that Frisky was now a hero.

Her mom thought JJ was a hero too because JJ may have saved their lives. JJ did ask her mom to promise not to go outside again if the oven was on. JJ's mom agreed.

STEP #9—ADD DIALOGUE

Now that you have written your draft, consider adding dialogue to make your story sound more realistic. This dialogue will also help your reader to hear directly the thoughts of those who are speaking.

Notice that when you write dialogue, you change the paragraph every time you change the speaker. Also, make sure that the dialogue fits the character who is speaking. A child on the playground will not sound like a college professor. At the same time, a parent should not be using language common to second graders.

JJ was worried. She didn't know what to do. She had never had to put out a fire before.

Suddenly, JJ remembered a conversation she had had with her Uncle Ralph, a fireman, at dinner last week.

JJ asked, "Should you throw water on a fire?"

Uncle Ralph replied, "Not if the fire is a grease fire—you know, like the ones in a kitchen."

Now that you have found some places in your story where you can include dialogue, proofread your work for mistakes the same way you did in the first chapter of this book when you wrote your persuasive essay. Also, look for places where you can add more detail.

Remember: when you write dialogue, you change the paragraph every time you change the speaker.

STEP #10—EDIT & SUBMIT YOUR ESSAY

Check Your Grammar and Spelling

Always check for grammar and spelling mistakes. By correcting these, you can give yourself a good chance of getting a higher score. An essay with good ideas but a lot of spelling and grammar mistakes will not receive a good score.

The first mistake is contained in the fourth sentence of the first paragraph. Instead of saying "She figured her mom would take care of business," the writer should say, "She figured her mom would solve the problem." Slang phrases should always be avoided in formal writing, especially on a test.

The next mistake is contained in the first sentence of the third paragraph: "As she walks out of her room, she was able to tell that the noise was being made by Frisky." You should not shift tenses in a paragraph. If you are writing in the past tense, then continue to write in the past tense. The verb "walks" should be "walked" since the entire paragraph is being written in the past tense.

Did you notice the third mistake? It is also contained in the third paragraph. It actually appears in the final sentence of the paragraph: "The barking was probably just Frisky's way of being psyched." The word "psyched" is slang. A better word to use would be "excited."

The next three mistakes are in the fourth paragraph. The first mistake in the paragraph is in first sentence: "When JJ got downstairs, however, she noticed that something was berning." The word "berning" should be spelled "burning."

For the next mistake in the paragraph, look at the second sentence: "JJ called to her mom to ask if nothing was wrong . . ." Instead of the word "nothing," the word "anything" should be used. There would not be a problem if "nothing" was wrong. JJ is concerned, however, since she is unsure if "anything was wrong".

The third and final mistake in the paragraph is contained in the last sentence: "JJ had to act quick." The word "quick" needs to be changed to "quickly" since the word being modified (to act) is a verb form. Only the adverb "quickly" and not the adjective "quick" can modify a verb form.

Check Your Content

Make sure that you also edit to improve the content of your essay. Let's return to the first paragraph of the sample essay draft. Concentrate on editing for content this time. Try to rewrite this paragraph to contain more specific detail. Think about the following questions:

1. What did JJ see when she opened her eyes?
2. What slang expression should the writer change?
3. In the last sentence, the author said, "How much louder could the noise become?" Is the noise the problem, or is there more to the situation?

Consider the first question: "What did JJ see when she opened her eyes?" Instead of saying, "JJ heard her alarm clock go off," it's more effective to say, "JJ looked at the alarm clock as she lay in bed." There's a combination of action and detail in the revised sentence.

Next, look at the second question: "What slang expression should the writer change?" The sentence "She figured her mom would take care of business, but she didn't" is weakened by the slang phrase "take care of business." This overused, stale phrase is an example of a cliché. As stated earlier, always avoid using clichés in your writing.

Finally, think about the quote mentioned in the third question: "How much louder could the noise become?" The loudness of the noise is not the issue in the story. Instead, the issue is Frisky's barking and scurrying, which fortunately wakes up JJ.

Submit Your Final Draft

Now it's time to submit your final draft. Give this writing your best effort. Make sure that you concentrate on the elements that we have discussed.

- Set the scene. Let your reader get close to the characters by
  - describing the way they look;
  - showing their traits;
  - "painting a word picture" that describes the characters and places in the scene.
- Introduce your conflict. Tell about
  - the problem that seems to be happening;
  - the reason that the situation being described is a problem.
- Decide the way in which the problem will be solved.
  - heroic action
  - unlikely happening
- Consider whether or not a lesson was learned by the main character(s).
  - If so, does the lesson make sense from the story you have written?
  - If not, does the story come to a definite conclusion?
- Think of a title that truly relates to your story. Be as specific as possible.

Speculative Story—Final Draft

Title _____

_____

_____

_____

_____

_____

_____

_____

(Please check page 238, in Chapter 8, Answer Keys and Explanations, for a corrected sample of this essay. Be sure to read the reason given for each correction. Your answers may be different. Make sure that all your suggestions are both correct and fitting for the essay.)

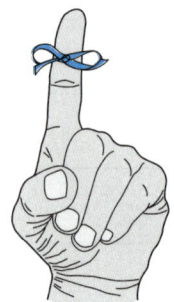

> ### Don't Forget to Follow the Guidelines
>
> Remember, when you write a story, always be sure to follow these guidelines.
>
> 1. Create the Realistic Main Conflict
> 2. Create the Plot (Plan of Action)
> 3. Create the Setting
> 4. Give Each Main Character a Personality
> 5. Develop the Story (Plot Line)
> 6. Write the Solution for the Problem (Resolve the Conflict)
> 7. Give Your Story a Working Title
> 8. Write Your First Draft
> 9. Add Dialogue
> 10. Edit and Submit Your Final Draft
>   a. Check Your Grammar and Spelling
>   b. Check Your Content
>   c. Hand in Your Final Draft

INDEPENDENT WRITING PRACTICE

Now that you have followed the entire writing process from beginning to end, it's time to practice your speculative writing skills by yourself. Use the space provided to pre-write. Organize your ideas by using the steps described above.

When you finish, check the **Suggested Main Points** listed on page 240 in the **Answer Key**. Your points may be just as good, if not better than the ones given.

TOPIC

You are walking along the street when you notice there is a large box wrapped in birthday paper. The tag on the box has a name written on it, but it's hard to read since it is a little smeared.

Think about the box that you have found. Now create a story and fill in the details of that story. Remember, your story should be based on events that most people would understand.

Do **not** simply describe what you see in your mind. Instead, make up a story about what is going on. You may wish to include some details that have happened even before the picture was taken.

Prewriting Space

Essay

Title: _____

Chapter 3

READING—LITERATURE

You'll complete two major tasks in this section of the test. First, you'll answer questions based on the passage. They'll deal with literary concepts like plot, character, and setting. Second, you'll write both brief and lengthy responses to questions also based on the passages. For these, you'll directly address the questions being raised. Your writing must demonstrate a high ability level.

Using the right strategies can help you to be very successful. We'll begin with the literary questions and move directly to the writing section.

USE THE PREVIEW TECHNIQUES (PT) TO BE SUCCESSFUL

Because these tests are timed, you might think that the best strategy is to read the passage and then answer the questions. Actually, that way is **NOT** the best way to take this test. Instead, use the **Preview Technique** (or **PT**) before you read each passage.

The Main Steps

Step #1—Preview the Questions
Read the questions given for the passage before you read the passage.

Step #2—Preview the Material
Skim through the essay and look for key words and phrases.

Step #3—Read the Entire Passage
Get all the information you'll need to answer the questions.

MAJOR TASK #1: ANSWER QUESTIONS BASED ON LITERATURE

For the Reading—Narrative section of the NJ ASK Language Arts Literacy Test for Grade 7, you'll answer questions based mostly short stories and poetry. Some questions will be based on the text, and others will be inferred (hinted at).

Let's do some practice exercises to improve your chances of doing well on this test. The following exercises contain questions featuring literary terms.

TARGET SKILLS 1-3: PLOT, CHARACTERS, AND SETTING

- **Plot** is the basic story line: the major events. The plot can be either simple or complex.
- **Characters** are the "players" in the work. The most important ones are main characters. Those who aren't as important are minor characters.
- **Setting** is the location in which the action takes place. When the action shifts to another place, the setting changes.

STRATEGY

- The minor events in the **plot** affect the major ones.
- **Characters** often have opposite points of view and different situations. These can help you to understand the reasons (motives) for the **characters'** actions.
- The **setting** helps the author get the main message (**theme**) across. For example, if the setting's peaceful, the author may want the actions to be peaceful.

Practice

The first passage we'll look at is from L. Frank Baum's classic novel, *The Wizard of Oz*. Even if you know the story well, you should still use the PT to help you to make the best decisions on your test. Be sure to:

> 1. Preview the questions.
> 2. Preview the material.
> 3. Read the entire passage.

THE WONDERFUL WIZARD OF OZ

by L. Frank Baum

Chapter 1. The Cyclone

Dorothy lived in the midst of the great Kansas prairies, with Uncle Henry, who was a farmer, and Aunt Em, who was the farmer's wife. Their house was small, for the lumber to build it had to be carried by wagon many miles. There were four walls, a floor and a roof, which made one room; and this room contained a rusty looking cookstove, a cupboard for the dishes, a table, three or four chairs, and the beds. Uncle Henry and Aunt Em had a big bed in one corner, and Dorothy a little bed in another corner. There was no garret at all, and no cellar—except a small hole dug in the ground, called a cyclone cellar, where the family could go in case one of those great whirlwinds arose, mighty enough to crush any building in its path. It was reached by a trap door in the middle of the floor, from which a ladder led down into the small, dark hole.

When Dorothy stood in the doorway and looked around, she could see nothing but the great gray prairie on every side. Not a tree nor a house broke the broad sweep of flat country that reached to the edge of the sky in all directions. The sun had baked the plowed land into a gray mass, with little cracks running through it. Even the grass was not green, for the sun had burned the tops of the long blades until they were the same gray color to be seen everywhere. Once the house had been painted, but the sun blistered the paint and the rains washed it away, and now the house was as dull and gray as everything else. When Aunt Em came there to live she was a young, pretty wife. The sun and wind had changed her, too. They had taken the sparkle from her eyes and left them a sober gray; they had taken the red from her cheeks and lips, and they were gray also. She was thin and gaunt, and never smiled now. When Dorothy, who was an orphan, first came to her, Aunt Em had been so startled by the child's laughter that she would scream and press her hand upon her heart whenever Dorothy's merry voice reached her ears; and she still looked at the little girl with wonder that she could find anything to laugh at.

Uncle Henry never laughed. He worked hard from morning till night and did not know what joy was. He was gray also, from his long beard to his rough boots, and he looked stern and solemn, and rarely spoke. It was Toto that made Dorothy laugh, and saved her from growing as gray as her other surroundings. Toto was not gray; he was a little black dog, with long silky hair and small black eyes that twinkled merrily on either side of his funny, wee nose. Toto played all day long, and Dorothy played with him, and loved him dearly.

Today, however, they were not playing. Uncle Henry sat upon the doorstep and looked anxiously at the sky, which was even grayer than usual. Dorothy stood in the door with Toto in her arms, and looked at the sky too. Aunt Em was washing the dishes.

From the far north they heard a low wail of the wind, and Henry and Dorothy could see where the long grass bowed in waves before the coming storm. There now came a sharp whistling in the air from the south, and as they turned their eyes that way they saw ripples in the grass coming from that direction also.

Suddenly Uncle Henry stood up. "There's a cyclone coming, Em," he called to his wife. "I'll go look after the stock." Then he ran toward the sheds where the cows and horses were kept.

Aunt Em dropped her work and came to the door. One glance told her of the danger close at hand.

"Quick, Dorothy!" she screamed. "Run for the cellar!"

Practice Questions

Answer the questions based on this passage using our **PT**. Circle each correct answer.

1. Which of these actions does **NOT** take place in this passage?

    A. Dorothy lived with her Uncle Henry and Aunt Em.

    B. Uncle Henry always laughed.

    C. Uncle Henry and Dorothy heard "a low wail of the wind" that came from the south.

    D. Aunt Em warned Dorothy to go in the cellar to protect herself from the cyclone that was coming.

2. Which of these events is out of sequence?

    A. Dorothy saw "nothing but the great gray prairie on every side" of her.

    B. Aunt Em warned Dorothy to "Run for the cellar!"

    C. Uncle Henry sat on the doorstep and looked anxiously at the sky.

    D. Uncle Henry "ran toward the shed where the cows and horses were kept."

3. What is the setting of the story?

    A. An orphanage.

    B. The mountains and prairies in Kansas.

    C. The eastern coast of the United States.

    D. The prairies in Kansas.

4. Which of these statements does **NOT** describe Uncle Henry?

   A. He always laughs.

   B. He works hard.

   C. His hair is gray.

   D. He is serious.

How do you think you did? Below, write down how many answers you think you've answered correctly.

I think I have answered ____ out of 4 questions correctly.

(Be sure to check your answers with those in the Answer Key, on page 240.)

MAJOR TASK #2: WRITING CLEAR, THOROUGH ESSAYS BASED ON READING PASSAGES

Next, you'll be writing short and long answers to selected questions. The short answers are scored "4" (high) to "0" (low). To earn a score of "4," you must answer the question thoroughly, support your main point(s) with details from the passage, add insight (thinking beyond obvious points), and use correct grammar, spelling, and vocabulary. A "2" is average. A "0" means the response either didn't answer the question or address the topic.

Short Essay for Plot, Character, and Setting

Describe Dorothy from this passage. Make sure that you only use information from the passage you have been given. Do not include any other details from the movie or book versions.

Pre-Writing Section
Use the space provided to make a writing plan for your essay.

Essay

Short Essay Grading Key

1. Thoroughly answered the question being asked. 4 3 2 1 0
2. Used enough supporting details in the essay. 4 3 2 1 0
3. Covered the topic completely and with insight. 4 3 2 1 0
4. Used correct grammar, spelling, and vocabulary. 4 3 2 1 0

Overall Grade 4 3 2 1 0

Scoring

4 Outstanding essay
3 Above-average writing with few mistakes
2 Average writing with some mistakes, little use of text, simple or false reasoning, and a simple writing style
1 Below-average writing with many mistakes, unclear references, too much opinion, and many grammar, vocabulary, and spelling errors
0 Poorly written response that didn't relate to the question, answer it directly, or address the topic

Be sure to check your answers against those in the Answer Key, page 241.

Long Essay for Plot, Character, and Setting

There are two possible answers for the following question. Use the scoring key below as your guideline.

The setting of this story is a farm in Kansas. Explain how the author uses the setting to show how difficult it must be to live there.

Pre-Writing Section
Use the space provided to make a writing plan for your essay.

Essay

Scoring

For the longer answers, the scores also range from a high of "4" points to a low of "0" points. To receive a "4," your essay needs to address the **4 Essay Keys**. Note: This essay simply needs more details since the question covers more.

4   Outstanding essay
3   Above-average writing with few mistakes
2   Average writing with some mistakes, little use of text, simple or false reasoning, and a simple writing style
1   Below-average writing with many mistakes, unclear references, too much opinion, and many grammar, vocabulary, and spelling errors
0   Poorly written response that didn't relate to the question, answer it directly, or address the topic

(As you finish each section, be sure to check your answers with those in the Answer Key, page 242.)

TARGET SKILLS 4, 5, AND 6: THEME, CAUSE AND EFFECT, AND POINT OF VIEW

- The **theme** is the main message that the author wants you to get while you're reading the work.
- Every event has at least one **cause** that results in an **effect**.
- **Point of view** deals either with the way a character sees things or the way a story is told. It's the "voice" that tells the story. A **first person narrator** tells the story in the "I" or "We" voice. A **second person narrator** tells the story in the "You" voice. A **third person narrator** tells the story using "she," "he," "it," or "they."

STRATEGY

- When you're looking for the **theme**, ask yourself the following questions:
  - What did I learn from this novel, story, or poem?
  - What has the author had the main characters do to show the theme?
  - Has the author made this point easy to see, or did (s)he hide it?

- Look to connect the **cause** with the **effect** that results. Phrases like "As a result" and "Therefore" help to make the connection.
- A **first person narrator** is a character who tells the story in the "I" or "We" voice. This allows you, the reader to be told the story by a character. A **second person narrator** speaks directly to "You" and often teaches a lesson. A **third person narrator** tells the story from someone who isn't usually part of the story.

Practice

The poem that we'll read is one that you may have seen before. It is *The Road Not Taken* by Robert Frost.

Read the poem thoroughly to help you to answer the questions as well as you can. Answer the questions based on this passage by using the **PT**. Be sure to:

> 1. Preview the questions.
> 2. Preview the material.
> 3. Read the entire passage.

THE ROAD NOT TAKEN

by Robert Frost

Two roads diverged in a yellow wood,
And sorry I could not travel both
And be one traveler, long I stood
And looked down one as far as I could
To where it bent in the undergrowth

Then took the other, as just as fair,
And having perhaps the better claim,
Because it was grassy and wanted wear;
Though as for that the passing there
Had worn them really about the same,

And both that morning equally lay
In leaves no step had trodden black.
Oh, I kept the first for another day!
Yet knowing how way leads on to way,
I doubted if I should ever come back.

> I shall be telling this with a sigh
> Somewhere ages and ages hence:
> Two roads diverged in a wood, and I—
> I took the one less traveled by,
> And that has made all the difference.

Practice Questions

Answer the questions based on this passage using our **PT**. Circle each correct answer.

1. From which point of view is the story of the poem being told?

    A. First person

    B. Second person

    C. Third person

    D. None of the above

2. What is the main idea in the first stanza (paragraph in poetry)?

    A. The traveler was lost.

    B. The traveler was hungry.

    C. The traveler was happy that he could travel both roads.

    D. The traveler was sad that he couldn't travel both roads.

3. The traveler hoped someday to take the road that "bent in the undergrowth", but what did he believe that the effect of his hopes would be?

    A. The traveler doubted he would take the other road some day.

    B. The traveler was sure he would take the other road some day.

    C. The traveler was paralyzed with fear.

    D. The traveler was encouraged by his friend to take the other road.

4. Which of these statements describes the main theme of the poem?

   A. The choice of the road taken happens in a dream.

   B. The choice of the road taken is a challenge.

   C. The choice of the road taken changes the traveler's life.

   D. The choice of the road taken frustrated the traveler.

How do you think you did? Below, write down how many answers you think you've answered correctly. After the review, go over any areas that gave you problems.

I think I have answered ___3___ out of 4 questions correctly.

(Be sure to check your answers with those in the Answer Key, on page 243.)

Short Essay for Theme, Cause and Effect, and Point of View

Briefly tell what the main idea is in the first stanza. Make sure that you only use information from the stanza.

Pre-Writing Section
Use the space provided to make a writing plan for your essay.

Essay

Now that you have finished writing, use the **4 Essay Keys** to give your work a grade.

Short Essay Grading Key

1. Thoroughly answered the question being asked.   4 3 2 1 0
2. Used enough supporting details in the essay.   4 3 2 1 0
3. Covered the topic completely and with insight.   4 3 2 1 0
4. Used correct grammar, spelling, and vocabulary.   4 3 2 1 0

Overall Grade 4 3 2 1 0

Scoring

4 Outstanding essay
3 Above-average writing with few mistakes
2 Average writing with some mistakes, little use of text, simple or false reasoning, and a simple writing style

1   Below-average writing with many mistakes, unclear references, too much opinion, and many grammar, vocabulary, and spelling errors

0   Poorly written response that didn't relate to the question, answer it directly, or address the topic

Be sure to check your answers against those in the Answer Key, page 244.

Long Essay for Theme, Cause and Effect, and Point of View

Write a summary of the poem. Be sure to include the main idea or event in each stanza. Also, look for a theme that goes beyond the obvious.

Pre-Writing Section
Use the space provided to make a writing plan for your essay.

Essay

Now that you have finished writing, use the **4 Essay Keys** to give your work a grade.

Long Essay Grading Key

1. Thoroughly answered the question being asked. 4 3 2 1 0
2. Used enough supporting details in the essay. 4 3 2 1 0
3. Covered the topic completely and with insight. 4 3 2 1 0
4. Used correct grammar, spelling, and vocabulary. 4 3 2 1 0

Overall Grade 4 3 2 1 0

Scoring

4 Outstanding essay
3 Above-average writing with few mistakes
2 Average writing with some mistakes, little use of text, simple or false reasoning, and a simple writing style
1 Below-average writing with many mistakes, unclear references, too much opinion, and many grammar, vocabulary, and spelling errors
0 Poorly written response that didn't relate to the question, answer it directly, or address the topic

(As you finish each section, be sure to check your answers with those in the Answer Key, page 244.)

TARGET SKILLS 7 AND 8: CONFLICT/RESOLUTION AND MAKING PREDICTIONS

- **Conflict**
  - The **conflict** refers to a problem. The main conflict is the main problem being faced by one or more of the protagonists (heroes) in the work.

- Resolution
  - The **resolution** is the solution to the conflict. When the conflict is resolved, the resolution isn't always one that the protagonist(s) may have wanted.
- **Making Predictions**
  - **Making predictions** helps you to use the information that you've read and to predict the action that's likely to take place.

STRATEGY

- The **conflict** should appear early in the work. One or more main characters are going to be challenged. This challenge will be the **main conflict**. In novels, there are often **minor conflicts** that make the **major conflict** appear even worse.
- The resolution happens when the problem is solved. Be sure to look for hints (**foreshadowing**) the author may give you to help you to guess the resolution. As you read the following passage, *The Queen Bee*, consider how the marble horses and the absence of men **foreshadow** the fate that will come to pass upon the two older brothers.
- Whether you **make predictions** about events likely to occur in the story or after the story ends, base them only on the story's information.

Practice

The fable that we'll read is *The Queen Bee* by the Brothers Grimm. It deals with the struggles faced by three brothers.

Read the fable thoroughly to help you to answer the questions as well as you can. Answer the questions based on this passage by using the **PT**. Be sure to:

> 1. Preview the questions.
> 2. Preview the material.
> 3. Read the entire passage.

THE QUEEN BEE

by The Brothers Grimm

Two kings' sons once upon a time went into the world to seek their fortunes; but they soon fell into a wasteful foolish way of living, so that they could not return home again. Then their brother, who was a little insignificant dwarf, went out to seek for his brothers: but when he had found them they only laughed at him, to think that he, who was so young and simple, should try to travel through the world, when they, who were so much wiser, had been unable to get on. However, they all set out on their journey together, and came at last to an ant hill. The two elder brothers would have pulled it down, in order to see how the poor ants in their fright would run about and carry off their eggs. But the little dwarf said, "Let the poor things enjoy themselves; I will not suffer you to trouble them."

So on they went, and came to a lake where many ducks were swimming about. The two brothers wanted to catch two, and roast them. But the dwarf said, "Let the poor things enjoy themselves; you shall not kill them." Next they came to a bees nest in a hollow tree, and there was so much honey that it ran down the trunk; and the two brothers wanted to light a fire under the tree and kill the bees so they could get their honey. But the dwarf held them back and said, 'Let the pretty insects enjoy themselves; I cannot let you burn them."

At length the three brothers came to a castle: and as they passed by the stables they saw fine horses standing there, but all were of marble, and no man was to be seen. Then they went through all the rooms, until they came to a door on which were three locks: but in the middle of the door was a wicket, so that they could look into the next room. There they saw a little grey old man sitting at a table; and they called to him once or twice, but he did not hear: however, they called a third time, and then he rose and came out to them.

He said nothing, but took hold of them and led them to a beautiful table covered with all sorts of good things; and when they had eaten and drunk, he showed each of them to a bed-chamber.

The next morning he came to the eldest and took him to a marble table, where there were three tablets, containing an account of the means by which the castle might be disenchanted. The first tablet said: "In the wood, under the moss, lie the thousand pearls belonging to the king's daughter; they must all be found: and if one be missing by set of sun, he who seeks them will be turned into marble."

The eldest brother set out, and sought for the pearls the whole day: but the evening came, and he had not found the first hundred: so he was turned into stone as the tablet had foretold.

The next day the second brother undertook the task; but he succeeded no better than the first; for he could only find the second hundred of the pearls; and therefore he too was turned into stone.

At last came the little dwarf's turn; and he looked in the moss; but it was so hard to find the pearls, and the job was so tiresome!—so he sat down upon a stone and cried.

And as he sat there, the king of the ants (whose life he had saved) came to help him, with five thousand ants; and it was not long before they had found all the pearls and laid them in a heap.

The second tablet said: "The key of the princess's bed-chamber must be fished up out of the lake." And as the dwarf came to the brink of it, he saw the two ducks whose lives he had saved swimming about; and they dived down and soon brought in the key from the bottom.

The third task was the hardest. It was to choose the youngest and the best of the king's three daughters. Now they were all beautiful, and all exactly alike: but he was told that the eldest had eaten a piece of sugar, the next some sweet syrup, and the youngest a spoonful of honey; so he was to guess which it was that had eaten the honey.

Then came the queen of the bees, who had been saved by the little dwarf from the fire, and she tried the lips of all three; but at last she sat upon the lips of the one that had eaten the honey: and so the dwarf knew which was the youngest. Thus the spell was broken, and all who had been turned into stones awoke, and took their proper forms. And the dwarf married the youngest and the best of the princesses, and was king after her father's death; but his two brothers married the other two sisters.

Practice Questions

Answer the questions based on this fable using our **PT**. Circle each correct answer.

1. Which of the brothers seems to shy away from conflict?

   A. The youngest (the dwarf)

   B. Second oldest

   C. Oldest

   D. All of the above

2. What is the conflict that the old man gives the oldest brother to resolve?

   A. Find the first hundred pearls or be turned into stone.

   B. Find all the missing pearls or be turned into stone.

   C. Find the dwarf or be turned into stone.

   D. Find the princess or be turned into stone.

3. When "The next day the second brother undertook the task," he:

   A. ran away.

   B. locked the old man in a prison and escaped with his brothers.

   C. accepted the challenge and succeeded.

   D. accepted the challenge and failed, also getting turned into stone.

4. Because the little brother (dwarf) had shown kindness to the ants, ducks, and bees, you can predict that:

   A. They would attack him because he's a dwarf.

   B. They would pay him money.

   C. They would run away because they're afraid of dwarfs.

   D. They would help him later in the story.

How do you think you did? Below, write down how many answers you think you've answered correctly. After the review, go over any areas that gave you problems.

I think I have answered 4 out of 4 questions correctly.

(Be sure to check your answers with those in the Answer Key, on page 245.)

Short Essay for Conflict/Resolution and Making Predictions

What is the reason (**cause**) that makes the older brothers fall into "a wasteful foolish way of living" when they go "into the world to seek their fortunes." How do the brothers react to their brother, the simple dwarf, when he goes out to find them? How can you predict their reaction? Make sure to cite at least one example from the text.

Pre-Writing Section
Use the space provided to make a writing plan for your essay.

Essay

Now that you have finished writing, use the **4 Essay Keys** to give your work a grade.

Short Essay Grading Key

1. Thoroughly answered the question being asked.	4	3	2	1	0
2. Used enough supporting details in the essay.	4	3	2	1	0
3. Covered the topic completely and with insight.	4	3	2	1	0
4. Used correct grammar, spelling, and vocabulary.	4	3	2	1	0

Overall Grade 4 3 2 1 0

Scoring

4 Outstanding essay
3 Above-average writing with few mistakes
2 Average writing with some mistakes, little use of text, simple or false reasoning, and a simple writing style
1 Below-average writing with many mistakes, unclear references, too much opinion, and many grammar, vocabulary, and spelling errors
0 Poorly written response that didn't relate to the question, answer it directly, or address the topic

Be sure to check your answers against those in the Answer Key, page 245.

Long Essay for Conflict/Resolution and Making Predictions

Explain how to "disenchant" (remove a magic spell from) the castle. The "little dwarf" was able to complete the three tasks written in the "three tablets" while his older brothers could not. Be sure to discuss the main conflict in the story that prevented the dwarf's older brothers from being successful. Also discuss the reason that the dwarf was able to complete the challenges that his brothers could not.

Pre-Writing Section
Use the space provided to make a writing plan for your essay.

Essay

Now that you have finished writing, use the **4 Essay Keys** to give your work a grade.

Long Essay Grading Key

1. Thoroughly answered the question being asked.	4	3	2	1	0
2. Used enough supporting details in the essay.	4	3	2	1	0
3. Covered the topic completely and with insight.	4	3	2	1	0
4. Used correct grammar, spelling, and vocabulary.	4	3	2	1	0

Overall Grade 4 3 2 1 0

Scoring

4 Outstanding essay
3 Above-average writing with few mistakes
2 Average writing with some mistakes, little use of text, simple or false reasoning, and a simple writing style
1 Below-average writing with many mistakes, unclear references, too much opinion, and many grammar, vocabulary, and spelling errors
0 Poorly written response that didn't relate to the question, answer it directly, or address the topic

(As you finish each section, be sure to check your answers with those in the Answer Key, page 246.)

TARGET SKILLS 9 AND 10: MOOD AND TONE

- **Mood**
  - Mood is the general feeling "in the air" in a work. The mood could be gloomy, realistic, hopeful, or even romantic.
- **Tone**
  - Tone is the attitude or way the speaker presents himself/herself. The tone could be serious, angry, happy, sad, or formal.

Reading—Literature

STRATEGY

- When reading, pretend that the narrator and main character(s) are speaking directly to you. As you listen to their words, consider how the situation feels to you. Is it hopeful? Are things dark and depressing? To find the mood, just listen to the way the story's being told.
- You can find the tone in a similar way. What emotions are the narrator and main character(s) feeling? Are they discussing serious issues, yelling during a fight, smiling, or speaking formally? These emotions reflect the work's tone.

Practice

The poem that we'll read is *The Children's Hour* by Henry Wadsworth Longfellow. The poet shares his thoughts about an evening spent while playing with his children, to whom he was very devoted.

Read the poem thoroughly to help to answer the questions. Answer the questions based on this poem by using the **PT**. Be sure to:

> 1. Preview the questions.
> 2. Preview the material.
> 3. Read the entire passage.

THE CHILDREN'S HOUR

by Henry Wadsworth Longfellow

Between the dark and the daylight,
When the night is beginning to lower,
Comes a pause in the day's occupations,
That is known as the Children's Hour.

I hear in the chamber above me
The patter of little feet,
The sound of a door that is opened,
And voices soft and sweet.

From my study I see in the lamplight,
Descending the broad hall stair,
Grave Alice, and laughing Allegra,
And Edith with golden hair.

A whisper, and then a silence:
Yet I know by their merry eyes
They are plotting and planning together
To take me by surprise.

A sudden rush from the stairway,
A sudden raid from the hall!
By three doors left unguarded
They enter my castle wall!

They climb up into my turret
O'er the arms and back of my chair;
If I try to escape, they surround me;
They seem to be everywhere.

They almost devour me with kisses,
Their arms about me entwine,
Till I think of the Bishop of Bingen
In his Mouse-Tower on the Rhine!

Do you think, o blue-eyed banditti,
Because you have scaled the wall,
Such an old mustache as I am
Is not a match for you all!

I have you fast in my fortress,
And will not let you depart,
But put you down into the dungeon
In the round-tower of my heart.

And there will I keep you forever,
Yes, forever and a day,
Till the walls shall crumble to ruin,
And moulder in dust away!

Practice Questions

Answer the questions based on this fable using our **PT**. Circle each correct answer.

1. Which of the following is **NOT** a possible tone of the poem's first four lines ("Between the dark and the daylight, When the night is beginning to lower, Comes a pause in the day's occupations, That is known as the Children's Hour")?

   A. Formal

   B. Clear

   C. Realistic

   D. Gloomy

2. What is the tone of lines 13–16 ("A whisper, and then a silence: Yet I know by their merry eyes—They are plotting and planning together—To take me by surprise")

   A. Nasty

   B. Playful

   C. Angry

   D. Sad

3. What is the tone of lines 29–32 ("Do you think, o blue-eyed banditti, Because you have scaled the wall, Such an old mustache as I am—Is not a match for you all!")?

   A. Angry

   B. Pompous

   C. Sad

   D. Challenging

4. When is the mood of Longfellow in lines 33–40 ("I have you fast in my fortress, And will not let you depart . . . Till the walls shall crumble to ruin, And moulder in dust away!").

   A. Worried

   B. Sad

   C. Playful

   D. Realistic

How do you think you did? Below, write down how many answers you think you've answered correctly. After the review, go over any areas that gave you problems.

I think I have answered ____ out of 4 questions correctly.

(Be sure to check your answers with those in the Answer Key, on page 246.)

Short Essay Question for Mood and Tone

Briefly explain what the tone of the poem is in the first four stanzas (paragraphs in poetry). Is Longfellow angry, serious, or sad? Is he formal, suspicious, or witty (clever)? Is the tone different than the choices mentioned?

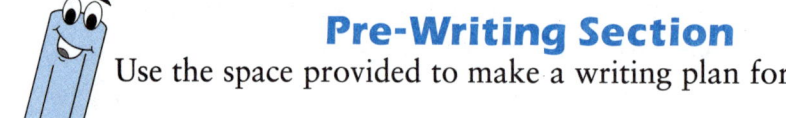

Pre-Writing Section

Use the space provided to make a writing plan for your essay.

Essay

Now that you have finished writing, use the **4 Essay Keys** to give your work a grade.

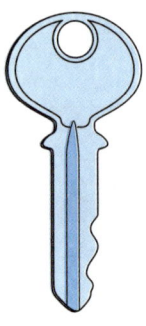

Short Essay Grading Key

1. Thoroughly answered the question being asked.   4 3 2 1 0
2. Used enough supporting details in the essay.   4 3 2 1 0
3. Covered the topic completely and with insight.   4 3 2 1 0
4. Used correct grammar, spelling, and vocabulary.   4 3 2 1 0

Overall Grade 4 3 2 1 0

Scoring

4 Outstanding essay
3 Above-average writing with few mistakes
2 Average writing with some mistakes, little use of text, simple or false reasoning, and a simple writing style
1 Below-average writing with many mistakes, unclear references, too much opinion, and many grammar, vocabulary, and spelling errors
0 Poorly written response that didn't relate to the question, answer it directly, or address the topic

(Be sure to check your answers with those in the Answer Key, on page 247.)

Long Essay for Mood and Tone

Explain how Longfellow uses mood in the poem. Is Longfellow feeling pessimistic? Is he playful? Are there other moods in the poem?

Pre-Writing Section

Use the space provided to make a writing plan for your essay.

Essay

Now that you have finished writing, use the **4 Essay Keys** to give your work a grade.

Long Essay Grading Key

1. Thoroughly answered the question being asked.	4	3	2	1	0
2. Used enough supporting details in the essay.	4	3	2	1	0
3. Covered the topic completely and with insight.	4	3	2	1	0
4. Used correct grammar, spelling, and vocabulary.	4	3	2	1	0

Overall Grade 4 3 2 1 0

Scoring

4 Outstanding essay
3 Above-average writing with few mistakes
2 Average writing with some mistakes, little use of text, simple or false reasoning, and a simple writing style
1 Below-average writing with many mistakes, unclear references, too much opinion, and many grammar, vocabulary, and spelling errors
0 Poorly written response that didn't relate to the question, answer it directly, or address the topic

(Be sure to check your answers with those in the Answer Key, on page 247.)

TARGET SKILLS 11–15: POETIC DEVICES—METAPHOR, SIMILE, PERSONIFICATION, RHYME AND SCHEME, AND ALLITERATION

- **Metaphor**
  - A metaphor shows how two objects or ideas are similar, even though they're usually not similar. For example, "The cloud is a soft pillow."
  - An extended metaphor "connects" two objects or ideas. Moreover, it's used throughout the work instead of in just one section.

- **Simile**
  - A simile also shows how two objects or ideas are similar, even though they're usually not similar. However, a simile uses "like" or "as" to make the comparison. A metaphor doesn't. For example, "The cloud is as soft as a pillow" or "She runs like a jaguar in the jungle."

- **Personification**
  - Personification gives human or living qualities to non-human or non-living things. For example, "The river sang a peaceful song of hope to the weary travelers."

- **Rhyme Scheme**
  - Rhyme scheme is the rhyming pattern in two or more lines of a stanza (poetry paragraph). Look at the last word in the line to find the rhyme. In the following example, notice that lines one and three rhyme. **Example:**
    I went to the park
    To play baseball.
    When it became dark
    I went home.

- **Alliteration**
  - Alliteration repeats the beginning sounds (usually consonants) of words that are close by. It can be used along with rhyme (see the first example). Also, alliteration can sometimes be used instead of rhyme (see the second example).

    First example:
    All the animals are alive.
    The forest has been saved by you five.

    Second example:
    Many more military men will receive medals
    this morning.
    Most of the militia will be honored.

STRATEGY

- Metaphors and similes add vivid description to literature.
  - They provide vivid descriptions. For example, "The cloud is (as soft as) a pillow."

- They use the traits of the object or idea in the comparison. For example, "She was as stubborn as a forged bar of steel" suggests that the girl's willpower is very strong.
- Metaphors and similes help you to see clearly the writer's images.

Personification adds life to descriptions. For example, "The ocean scolded the fishermen by slapping their boats with its powerful waves and roaring disapproval."

Practice

As you read Joyce Kilmer's poem, *Trees*, notice Kilmer's use of metaphor, simile, and personification. Also, look for an extended metaphor.

Read the poem thoroughly to help to answer the questions. Answer the questions based on this poem by using the **PT**. Be sure to:

1. Preview the questions.
2. Preview the material.
3. Read the entire passage.

Trees

By Joyce Kilmer

I think that I shall never see
A poem lovely as a tree.

A tree whose hungry mouth is prest (pressed)
Against the earth's sweet flowing breast;

A tree that looks at God all day,
And lifts her leafy arms to pray;

A tree that may in Summer wear
A nest of robins in her hair;

Upon whose bosom snow has lain;
Who intimately lives with rain.

Poems are made by fools like me,
But only God can make a tree.

Practice Questions

Answer the questions based on this poem using our PT. Circle each correct answer.

1. The simile used in line two of the poem compares the poem to what object?

    A. a tree

    B. grass

    C. a mouth

    D. robins

2. In line 3 of the poem, what is the tree's "hungry mouth" allowing it to do?

    A. speak

    B. cry

    C. get nourishment

    D. yawn

3. In line six of the poem, "And lifts her leafy arms to pray" is an example of what literary device(s)?

    A. metaphor

    B. personification

    C. alliteration

    D. all of the above

4. Lines seven and eight of the poem state, "A tree that may in Summer wear / A nest of robins in her hair." These lines are an example of what literary device(s)?

    A. metaphor

    B. simile

    C. personification

    D. both "A" and "C"

How do you think you did? Write down how many answers you think you've answered correctly. After the review, go over any areas that gave you problems.

I think I have answered __2__ out of 4 questions correctly.

(Be sure to check your answers with those in the Answer Key, on page 247.)

Short Essay for Metaphor, Simile, Personification, Rhyme Scheme, and Alliteration

Consider lines seven and eight in Kilmer's **Trees:** "A tree that may in Summer wear / A nest of robins in her hair." Explain how Kilmer uses metaphor and personification in these lines.

Pre-Writing Section
Use the space provided to make a writing plan for your essay.

Essay

Now that you have finished writing, use the **4 Essay Keys** to give your work a grade.

Short Essay Grading Key

1.	Thoroughly answered the question being asked.	4	3	2	1	0
2.	Used enough supporting details in the essay.	4	3	2	1	0
3.	Covered the topic completely and with insight.	4	3	2	1	0
4.	Used correct grammar, spelling, and vocabulary.	4	3	2	1	0

Overall Grade 4 3 2 1 0

Scoring

4   Outstanding essay
3   Above-average writing with few mistakes
2   Average writing with some mistakes, little use of text, simple or false reasoning, and a simple writing style
1   Below-average writing with many mistakes, unclear references, too much opinion, and many grammar, vocabulary, and spelling errors
0   Poorly written response that didn't relate to the question, answer it directly, or address the topic

(Be sure to check your answers against those in the Answer Key, page 248.)

Long Essay for Metaphor, Simile, Personification, Rhyme Scheme, and Alliteration

Explain how Kilmer has written *Trees* as an extended metaphor. Be sure to include the use of metaphor and simile throughout the poem. Explain how the use of rhyme affects the tone of the poem.

Pre-Writing Section
Use the space provided to make a writing plan for your essay.

Essay

Now that you have finished writing, use the **4 Essay Keys** to give your work a grade.

Long Essay Grading Key

1. Thoroughly answered the question being asked.	4	3	2	1	0
2. Used enough supporting details in the essay.	4	3	2	1	0
3. Covered the topic completely and with insight.	4	3	2	1	0
4. Used correct grammar, spelling, and vocabulary.	4	3	2	1	0

Overall Grade 4 3 2 1 0

Scoring

4   Outstanding essay
3   Above-average writing with few mistakes
2   Average writing with some mistakes, little use of text, simple or false reasoning, and a simple writing style
1   Below-average writing with many mistakes, unclear references, too much opinion, and many grammar, vocabulary, and spelling errors
0   Poorly written response that didn't relate to the question, answer it directly, or address the topic

(As you finish each section, be sure to check your answers with those in the Answer Key, page 248.)

Chapter 4

INFORMATIONAL (EVERYDAY) READING

In English class, you read many poems, stories, novels, grammar exercises, and more. Both in your other classes and outside of school, you're may be reading newspapers, magazines, e-mails, IM's (Instant Messages), and other printed material. This is **informational (everyday) reading**.

Because reading is so important, you must practice to keep sharp. Reading every day can actually help you to be a better reader.

To answer questions in this category, you must read the passages carefully. Before you do so, you will continue to use the **PT (Preview Technique) Strategy**.

Be sure to:

1. **Preview the questions you actually need to answer.**
2. **Preview the material.**
3. **Read the entire passage to find key lines or phrases that relate to the questions.**

This section of the NJ ASK Language Arts Grade 7 Test will give you reading selections found in textbooks, magazines, reference books, or other sources. Even though you may find a topic or person that you don't know a lot about, read the entire passage carefully since the questions are based on the passage.

Here are some practice exercises to improve your chances of doing well on this test. Let's concentrate on some of the everyday reading skills that you'll be tested on.

TARGET SKILLS 1 AND 2: DETAILS AND SEQUENCE OF EVENTS

- Reading passages always have **details**, the facts that explain the information you're reading.
- The **sequence of events** is the order in which things happen.

STRATEGY

- When looking for **details**, concentrate on the facts and **not** on opinions.
- When looking for the **sequence of events**:
  - Look for transition words and phrases like "first," "next," and "the final step."
  - Look for numbers or bullet points to guide you.
  - Look for the abbreviations "AM" and "PM" for time sequences.

Practice

The passage is entitled *Things Had Really Changed!* It deals with a young boy who doesn't start out being happy on the first day of school. Use only facts from the passage to answer each question.

Read the passage thoroughly to help to answer the questions. Answer the questions based on this passage by using the PT. Be sure to:

> 1. Preview the questions.
> 2. Preview the material.
> 3. Read the entire passage.

THINGS HAD REALLY CHANGED!

When Jonathan had walked into his 7th grade homeroom on the last day of class in school, he wasn't as happy as he thought he would be. Yes, he loved the freedom in the summer. He wouldn't have to follow a schedule every day. On the first day of school in September, Jonathan had quickly written a note in his planner as he sat down at his desk. The note said, "Only 179 more days to go until summer comes back!" He never expected that he might actually enjoy school this year.

Jonathan's previous years in school had not been that bad, but they also weren't great.

He got into trouble sometimes, but he had never been suspended. He always knew when to stop his fooling around with his friends.

He didn't think that he would like any of his classes this year, but he was actually wrong. He found that he liked Miss Rumson's English class the best. She had encouraged him to write when he was in central detention with her last year. She had looked at some of his writing and even laughed at his story about falling off his bike while showing off to his friends.

Things would get even better in Miss Rumson's class. After he had handed in his first assignment, she told him that he has a lot of writing talent. A lot of teachers had said that to Jonathan before, but this was different somehow. Miss Rumson seemed to take a personal interest in Jonathan's writing.

For the first month of school, Miss Rumson tried to get Jonathan to join the school newspaper. He resisted at first, but Miss Rumson was persistent. Finally, he agreed and was assigned to cover the school's wrestling matches. Jonathan had never gone to a school event before because his friends would think he wasn't "cool." That's the reason why he didn't tell his friends that he was going.

When he was at the first match, he noticed that the head cheerleader, Katie, smiled at him. He smiled back, but he didn't think anything about it. When his story came out about the school team's first win of the year, Jonathan knew that his friends would make fun of him. Actually, that didn't happen because the captain of the team was also the brother of one of his good friends.

School really began to change for Jonathan. He started to take his books home every night. Sometimes he went out with his friends instead of studying, but there were times when he actually did study. After one of those times when he studied, he received the second highest grade on Miss Rumson's test. Who had received the top grade? Katie earned a perfect score, of course.

His friends teased Jonathan a little more for his high score on the test, but he didn't get as upset about it as he had thought he would. In fact, something good happened. Katie asked him if he would study with her for the next test. Jonathan was shocked, but he was also very pleased.

Jonathan believed that no one had ever thought that he was a good student. He remembered that his fourth grade teacher had told him he could be a very good student if he would just work a little harder. He hadn't listened because most of his friends didn't study. Jonathan hadn't wanted to lose his friends.

Things were different now. Jonathan was on the school newspaper. The older brother of one of his friends was on the team so Jonathan wouldn't be teased for covering the wrestlers for the school newspaper. More importantly, the head cheerleader, Katie, wanted to study with him.

Two weeks later, Jonathan had become a little uneasy. When he had arrived home after school, his mom mentioned that Miss Rumson had called. Even though he didn't remember doing anything wrong in school, he was ready to apologize. He figured that he must have done something wrong. Why else would the teacher be calling?

Well, things couldn't have been better for Jonathan. He learned that he had received the highest grade in the class on the last test. His grade was actually one point higher than Katie's. He also learned that Miss Rumson liked his reporting skills so much that she had contacted the local newspaper. The editor said that he would be willing to take Jonathan's reports about the school wrestling team and place them in the paper.

Jonathan had not been very happy when the school year had started. Now, he looked at things completely differently. The next day, Jonathan wrote in his planner that 7th grade wasn't so bad.

Practice Questions

Answer the questions based on this passage using our **PT**. Circle each correct answer.

1. Starting with Jonathan's first day in 7th grade, which event is out of sequence?

   A. First, "Jonathan had quickly written a note in his planner as he sat down at his desk."

   B. Second, Jonathan "was assigned to cover the school's wrestling matches."

   C. Third, Jonathan "had received the highest grade in the class on the last test."

   D. All events are listed in sequence.

2. During all his years in school, how many times had Jonathan been suspended?

   A. None

   B. One

   C. Two

   D. Five

3. Why didn't Jonathan tell his friends that he was covering the wrestling team?

   A. His best friend had been thrown off the team.

   B. He thought his friends wouldn't think he was "cool."

   C. He thought Katie wouldn't think he was "cool."

   D. He thought his teachers wouldn't think he was "cool."

4. For what group did Jonathan cover the wrestling team?

   A. The principal's newsletter.

B. The parent-teacher group's newsletter.

C. The class newspaper.

D. The school newspaper.

How do you think you did? Below, write down how many answers you think you've answered correctly. After the review, go over any areas that gave you problems.

I think I have answered ____ out of 4 questions correctly.

(Be sure to check your answers against those in the Answer Key, page 248.)

Short Essay for Details and Sequence of Events

Explain how Jonathan knew Miss Rumson before the first day of 7th grade?

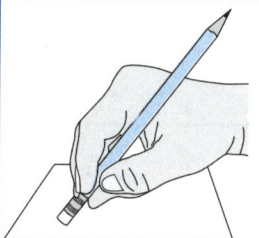

Pre-Writing Section

Use the space provided to make a writing plan for your essay.

Essay

Now that you have finished writing, use the **4 Essay Keys** to give your work a grade.

Short Essay Grading Key

1.	Thoroughly answered the question being asked.	4	3	2	1	0
2.	Used enough supporting details in the essay.	4	3	2	1	0
3.	Covered the topic completely and with insight.	4	3	2	1	0
4.	Used correct grammar, spelling, and vocabulary.	4	3	2	1	0

Overall Grade 4 3 2 1 0

Scoring

4   Outstanding essay
3   Above-average writing with few mistakes
2   Average writing with some mistakes, little use of text, simple or false reasoning, and a simple writing style
1   Below-average writing with many mistakes, unclear references, too much opinion, and many grammar, vocabulary, and spelling errors
0   Poorly written response that didn't relate to the question, answer it directly, or address the topic

(Be sure to check your answers against those in the Answer Key, page 249.)

Long Essay for Details and Sequence of Events

Explain how "School really began to change for Jonathan."

Pre-Writing Section
Use the space provided to make a writing plan for your essay.

Essay

Informational (Everyday) Reading • 117

Now that you have finished writing, use the **4 Essay Keys** to give your work a grade.

Long Essay Grading Key

1.	Thoroughly answered the question being asked.	4	3	2	1	0
2.	Used enough supporting details in the essay.	4	3	2	1	0
3.	Covered the topic completely and with insight.	4	3	2	1	0
4.	Used correct grammar, spelling, and vocabulary.	4	3	2	1	0

Overall Grade 4 3 2 1 0

Scoring

4 Outstanding essay
3 Above-average writing with few mistakes
2 Average writing with some mistakes, little use of text, simple or false reasoning, and a simple writing style
1 Below-average writing with many mistakes, unclear references, too much opinion, and many grammar, vocabulary, and spelling errors
0 Poorly written response that didn't relate to the question, answer it directly, or address the topic

(As you finish each section, be sure to check your answers with those in the Answer Key, page 249.)

TARGET SKILL 3: CENTRAL IDEA OR THEME

The **central idea or theme** in a passage tells you what the main topic is. A passage about a famous mountain climber, for example, may feature the courage of the climber as the **central idea or theme.**

STRATEGY

As you are reading a chapter in your textbook, an article on the Internet, or a story about a famous person, try these strategies to help you to find the **central idea or theme.**

- Look at the title since it may often contain the **central idea or theme.**
- Look at the first sentence in the first paragraph. It may either contain the theme or be leading you directly to it.
- Look for a summary or a closing comment at the end of the passage, as well.

Practice

The passage that we'll read is entitled *Vacation*. It is an article about the places in New Jersey where you can go to take a vacation.

Read the passage thoroughly to help to answer the questions. Answer the questions based on this passage by using the **PT**. Be sure to:

> 1. Preview the questions.
> 2. Preview the material.
> 3. Read the entire passage.

Vacation

Many of us travel long distances to take our vacations. Even though it's nice to travel, did you know that you could take a vacation without leaving our state of New Jersey? Whether we like the mountains, the ocean, shopping or sightseeing, there are many interesting attractions to see throughout the state. New Jersey is your in-state vacation spot.

If the mountains interest you, then visit the Delaware Water Gap in the northwest section of the state. They have hiking trails, boating, fishing, beautiful scenery, and more. If you head to the Skylands area in the northwest, be sure to visit in the winter. You'll find many skiing, snowboarding, and sledding areas where you can burn off some of that extra energy. Don't forget the reservoirs throughout the state that provide some of the same activities as the ones you can find in the Delaware Water Gap and the Skylands.

On a hot summer day, head for the Jersey shore. Explore miles and miles of sandy beaches where you can swim or get a tan. Get a few friends and ride your boogie board. Take a walk and enjoy the shops, the saltwater taffy, the Italian ice treats, and the amusements on the boardwalk in Atlantic City. You can even take a ride on an old-fashioned paddlewheel boat in Tom's River, Beach Haven, and Point Pleasant Beach.

If you're into sports, New Jersey has the Meadowlands Complex. This is the home of various professional sports teams including football's Giants and Jets, basketball's Nets, hockey's Devils, and Soccer's Red Bulls. Baseball fans can take in a game at eight different professional league parks. The teams that play there include the Trenton Thunder, the Somerset Patriots, and the New Jersey Jackals. If you like auto racing, visit one of the auto racetracks that sponsor NASCAR and NHRA races in towns like New Egypt and Old Bridge. Throughout New Jersey, there are also many public parks that have sports fields and tennis courts for you to enjoy.

If you like history, there are many places to visit throughout the state. For example, in the northeast Gateway region, places of interest include the Edison National Historic Site in West Orange and President Grover Cleveland's birthplace in Caldwell. In the Skylands region, check out the Fosterfields Living History Farm in Morris Plains and the Elias Van Bunschooten (Colonial) Museum in Sussex. The Delaware region has Batsto (Colonial) Village in Batsto and the C. A. Nothnagle Log House in Gibbstown. Be sure to remember to check out the many lighthouses throughout the Shore regions. Finally, visit the NJ Vietnam Veterans' Memorial in Holmdel and pay tribute to our soldiers who lost their lives in defense of our country.

New Jersey provides a lot of variety for your vacations, and you never have to leave the state. Whether you're looking for amusement rides, majestic mountains, sandy beaches, sports, or history, you can find them in your own home state. Remember to think of New Jersey, your in-state vacation spot, when you're planning your next vacation.

Practice Questions

Answer the questions based on this passage using our **PT**. Circle each correct answer.

1. Which of these titles would relate more closely to the **central idea or theme**?

   A. My Vacation

   B. Where to Take a Vacation

   C. New Jersey Vacations for New Jersey Residents

   D. Vacations for All Seasons

2. What is the main point of the third paragraph?

   A. It's hot at the seashore.

   B. The New Jersey seashore has swimming, shopping, food, and more.

   C. All of the historic areas are located at the New Jersey seashore.

   D. The New Jersey seashore doesn't get many visitors in the winter.

3. Which of these statements is a detail that does **NOT** support the central idea or theme in the fourth paragraph?

   A. The Meadowlands Complex is the home of various professional sports teams.

   B. There are eight different professional league parks for baseball.

   C. There are swimming pools in many towns.

   D. There are auto racetracks that sponsor NASCAR and NHRA races.

4. Which of these statements is a detail that does **NOT** support the central idea or theme in the fifth paragraph?

   A. The NJ Vietnam Veterans' Memorial is located near the Garden State Parkway.

   B. The Edison National Historic Site in located in West Orange.

   C. The Fosterfields Living History Farm is located in Morris Plains.

   D. The C. A. Nothnagle Log House is located in Gibbstown.

How do you think you did? Below, write down how many answers you think you've answered correctly. After the review, go over any areas that gave you problems.

I think I have answered ___4___ out of 4 questions correctly.

(Be sure to check your answers against those in the Answer Key, page 250.)

Informational (Everyday) Reading

Short Essay for Central Idea or Theme

What is the **central idea or theme** in the second paragraph?

Pre-Writing Section
Use the space provided to make a writing plan for your essay.

Essay

Now that you have finished writing, use the **4 Essay Keys** to give your work a grade.

Short Essay Grading Key

1.	Thoroughly answered the question being asked.	4	3	2	1	0
2.	Used enough supporting details in the essay.	4	3	2	1	0
3.	Covered the topic completely and with insight.	4	3	2	1	0
4.	Used correct grammar, spelling, and vocabulary.	4	3	2	1	0

Overall Grade 4 3 2 1 0

Scoring

4   Outstanding essay
3   Above-average writing with few mistakes
2   Average writing with some mistakes, little use of text, simple or false reasoning, and a simple writing style
1   Below-average writing with many mistakes, unclear references, too much opinion, and many grammar, vocabulary, and spelling errors
0   Poorly written response that didn't relate to the question, answer it directly, or address the topic

(Be sure to check your answers against those in the Answer Key, page 250.)

Long Essay for Central Idea or Theme

State the **central idea or theme** of the entire article. Be sure to use specific examples to explain your answer.

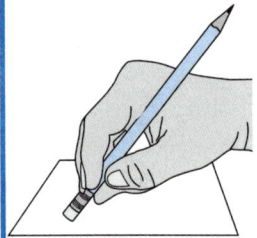

Pre-Writing Section
Use the space provided to make a writing plan for your essay.

Essay

Now that you have finished writing, use the **4 Essay Keys** to give your work a grade.

Long Essay Grading Key

1. Thoroughly answered the question being asked.   4 3 2 1 0
2. Used enough supporting details in the essay.   4 3 2 1 0
3. Covered the topic completely and with insight.   4 3 2 1 0
4. Used correct grammar, spelling, and vocabulary.   4 3 2 1 0

Overall Grade 4 3 2 1 0

Scoring

4 Outstanding essay
3 Above-average writing with few mistakes
2 Average writing with some mistakes, little use of text, simple or false reasoning, and a simple writing style
1 Below-average writing with many mistakes, unclear references, too much opinion, and many grammar, vocabulary, and spelling errors
0 Poorly written response that didn't relate to the question, answer it directly, or address the topic

(As you finish each section, be sure to check your answers with those in the Answer Key, page 250.)

TARGET SKILLS 4-6: QUESTIONING, CLARIFYING, AND PREDICTING

Questioning is the effective use of questions to gather information. **Clarifying** is the way to find out further information about a topic. **Predicting** is making educated guesses based on both the information that you have already found out and information that you already know.

STRATEGY

As you are doing your reading, use these strategies.

- For effective **Questioning**, make sure that your questions are designed to bring you the information that you seek. Be specific.
- Use specific questions when you need help **Clarifying** information.
- When you are **Predicting**, make sure that your predictions are based on logic and common sense.

Practice

The passage that we'll read is a 7th grade student's journal entry entitled *My First Day of School*. The following questions deal with **Questioning, Clarifying, and Predicting**.

Read the passage thoroughly to help to answer the questions. Answer the questions based on this passage by using the **PT**. Be sure to:

1. Preview the questions.
2. Preview the material.
3. Read the entire passage.

MY FIRST DAY OF SCHOOL

by Pat Cole

When I set my alarm last night, I realized that tomorrow I would be following a different routine for the next few months. Since school had let out last June, I suddenly had a lot more freedom. I could sleep a little later, eat lunch whenever I wanted to, watch my favorite daytime television programs, and just hang out with my friends. Tomorrow morning, it was time to go back to school.

The next morning, my mom woke me up even before my alarm rang. She told me that I had to make sure that I was awake. I couldn't go back to sleep. If I did, I would be late for the first day of school. She said, "That's not the way you want to start out your school year, is it?" I just grumbled "No" and slid out of my bed.

I found my way to the bathroom and jumped in the shower. During the summer, I never had to take my shower before breakfast. I always made some cereal, poured a glass of juice, and settled in with my favorite television program on one of the music channels. Today, however, I had to finish my shower, dry my hair, and have a little breakfast. Oh, I couldn't do these things in slow motion. My mom kept reminded me to "Hurry up!" so I wouldn't be late. She also reminded me to wear the new outfit we had bought last week. "You should always make a good first impression, especially on the first day of school," she said. It would feel funny dressing up for breakfast after an entire summer of eating while wearing my pajamas.

My mom made me hot cereal, toast, and juice for breakfast. She also cut up some melon for me. I was still a little tired and didn't feel like eating much. My mom told me that I would be hungry before lunch if I didn't eat a good breakfast, but I just wasn't hungry. Besides, lunch was only a few hours away, wasn't it?

After I had finished my breakfast, I walked out the door. I noticed that my skateboard was hanging from the hook near the door. I wonder what would happen if I took my skateboard and rode it one last time down my driveway. The bus isn't due for another minute. Besides, aren't the buses always late on the first day? Oh, it's just my luck. Here's comes the bus—right on schedule.

Well, I least I'm getting to be with my friends on the ride to school. We talk about all the things we always talk about, but it's different today. Before we know it, the bus pulls up to the school. We all get off and head to our homerooms.

Classes aren't too bad. Miss Washington is still greeting every one of her students at her front door. Vice-Principal Palmer is disciplining a rowdy student for getting in trouble near the lockers. I only have to carry my math and public speaking textbooks this year because most of our classes let us keep an extra book at home.

Things actually didn't go too badly all throughout my day, but I did have one little problem. Around ten o'clock in the morning, I was hungry. Lunch wasn't on my schedule until noon. I had to sit in three different classes and listen to my stomach reminding me that I should have eaten my breakfast. What's worse is we had a discussion in English class of the ways fast food restaurants try to sell us their burgers, fries, tacos, and chicken. I could almost hear the food calling me by my name.

After I had lunch, the rest of the day seemed to fly by. I enjoyed my social studies class because Mr. Barns is a great guy. He doesn't hassle his students, and he never makes fun of anyone in his class. Gym was great because I got to blow off a little steam. Miss Springer let us choose an activity today, so my friends and I played dodgeball.

When the day was over, I got on the bus and headed home. I didn't think it was fair that we were assigned a one-page journal entry in English class, but I guess I can finish by just writing about my day.

Boy, I hope the weekend gets here quickly. I'm going to sleep late on Saturday.

Practice Questions

Answer the questions based on this passage using our **PT**. Circle each correct answer.

1. What do you think was Pat's attitude after setting the alarm for the morning of the first day of school?

   A. Happy because the summer was boring.

   B. Afraid because the school was in a different town.

   C. Upset because there would be less freedom in school.

   D. Excited to be with friends again.

2. What could you predict when Pat used the excuse "lunch was only a few hours away, wasn't it?" to disregard mom's advice to eat a good breakfast?

   A. Pat's mom would be right.

   B. Pat would be right.

   C. Pat's brother would be right.

   D. All of the above.

3. If Pat had taken his skateboard and ridden it "one last time down (his) driveway" before the bus came, why might Pat's mom be upset?

   A. Pat's new clothes might be ruined.

   B. Pat might get hurt and miss the first day of school.

   C. Pat might miss the bus.

   D. All of the above.

4. During the morning of the second day of school, what is Pat likely to do?

   A. Sleep late

   B. Eat breakfast while wearing pajamas and sitting in front of the television

   C. Eat a good breakfast

   D. Walk the dog

How do you think you did? Below, write down how many answers you think you've answered correctly.

I think I have answered _____ out of 4 questions correctly.

(Be sure to check your answers against those in the Answer Key, page 251. After the review, go over any areas that gave you problems.)

Short Essay for Questioning, Clarifying, and Predicting

Explain why Pat's mother would be upset if Pat were late for school.

Pre-Writing Section

Use the space provided to make a writing plan for your essay.

Essay

Now that you have finished writing, use the **4 Essay Keys** to give your work a grade.

Short Essay Grading Key

1.	Thoroughly answered the question being asked.	4	3	2	1	0
2.	Used enough supporting details in the essay.	4	3	2	1	0
3.	Covered the topic completely and with insight.	4	3	2	1	0
4.	Used correct grammar, spelling, and vocabulary.	4	3	2	1	0

Overall Grade 4 3 2 1 0

Scoring

4   Outstanding essay
3   Above-average writing with few mistakes
2   Average writing with some mistakes, little use of text, simple or false reasoning, and a simple writing style
1   Below-average writing with many mistakes, unclear references, too much opinion, and many grammar, vocabulary, and spelling errors
0   Poorly written response that didn't relate to the question, answer it directly, or address the topic

(Be sure to check your answers against those in the Answer Key, page 251.)

Long Essay for Questioning, Clarifying, and Predicting

Predict how the rest of the school year is expected to go for Pat. Use information from the essay to support your predictions.

Pre-Writing Section

Use the space provided to make a writing plan for your essay.

Essay

Now that you have finished writing, use the **4 Essay Keys** to give your work a grade.

Long Essay Grading Key

1.	Thoroughly answered the question being asked.	4	3	2	1	0
2.	Used enough supporting details in the essay.	4	3	2	1	0
3.	Covered the topic completely and with insight.	4	3	2	1	0
4.	Used correct grammar, spelling, and vocabulary.	4	3	2	1	0

Overall Grade 4 3 2 1 0

Scoring

4   Outstanding essay
3   Above-average writing with few mistakes
2   Average writing with some mistakes, little use of text, simple or false reasoning, and a simple writing style
1   Below-average writing with many mistakes, unclear references, too much opinion, and many grammar, vocabulary, and spelling errors
0   Poorly written response that didn't relate to the question, answer it directly, or address the topic

(As you finish each section, be sure to check your answers with those in the Answer Key, page 252.)

TARGET SKILL 7: FACT VERSUS OPINION

A **Fact** is information that can be measured and proven. An **Opinion** shows the way someone feels about a **Fact**.

STRATEGY

As you are doing your reading, use these strategies.

- A fact is something that is easy to measure and prove.
  - Look for measurements for proof (for example, *gallons*, *days*, and *inches*).
  - Look for quotes and citations from books and newspapers.
- An opinion is an interpretation.
  - Look for key words or phrases, such as *Sometimes* or *As I see it*.

Practice

The passage that we'll read is a 7th grade student's letter to the mayor of her town. The questions that follow deal with **Fact versus Opinion**.

Read the passage thoroughly to help to answer the questions. Answer the questions based on this passage by using the **PT**. Be sure to:

> 1. Preview the questions.
> 2. Preview the material.
> 3. Read the entire passage.

A LETTER TO THE MAYOR

March 25, 2007

Dear Mayor Patel,

   I believe that we should have a place in town where all the kids can get together. The park near the river used to have a building where we could play games or just sit with our friends and talk. There was even some blacktop where we used to roller skate or ride our skateboards. Now, the building is closed because there's no one to take care of it. Mr. Ross used to volunteer his time on the weekends to make sure the building was kept up for us kids, but he retired and moved to Florida.

   A meeting place for us kids is a great idea for our town. Right now, we have no place to go where we can be with our friends. When we go to the movies, the security guards are mean to us. They're always chasing us away. Sometimes, they even holler at us for laughing too loudly. How can we help it if something's funny? Don't you laugh out loud sometimes, too?

Every time we ask for a meeting place for us teens, we're told that large groups of teens cause trouble. Why do people say this to us? We don't look for trouble. Now, I know that some kids can cause problems, but that's why there are adults to watch us. If you put a large group of adults together, don't you think that some of them would get in trouble too? If you don't believe me, just look at the police records for the past month. Are teens the only ones causing trouble?

Last month when we came to a town council meeting to ask for a teen center, you became upset with us. You told us that there were too many kids hanging out in the Maple Grove Shopping Center parking lot behind the movie theater. You told us that you were concerned that nine teenagers had been arrested for fighting during the last month. That may be so, but those kids don't represent all of us in town who really want a place to go at night. If you gave us a teen center, there wouldn't be any more trouble in town because we'd be off the streets. We'd all want to be with our friends.

Please reconsider my request for a teen center in town. It's a place we really need. Without it, we'll probably just keep having trouble in town.

Sincerely,
Victoria Martinez

Practice Questions

Answer the questions based on this passage using our **PT**. Circle each correct answer.

1. Which of the following statements is a fact?

   A. Victoria Martinez wrote the letter to Mayor Patel.

   B. Victoria Martinez wrote the letter to her friends.

   C. Mayor Patel wrote the letter to Victoria Martinez and her friends.

   D. Mayor Patel wrote the letter to Victoria Martinez.

2. Which of these statements is **NOT** a fact?

   A. "I believe that we should have a place in town …"

   B. "… the building is closed."

   C. "Mr. Ross used to volunteer his time on the weekends."

   D. Mr. Ross "retired and moved to Florida."

3. Which of these statements is a fact?

   A. The security guards are "always chasing us away."

   B. "... the security guards are mean to us."

   C. "... we go to the movies."

   D. "... large groups of teens cause trouble."

4. Which of these statements is an opinion?

   A. "... we came to a town council meeting."

   B. "... there were too many kids hanging out in the Maple Grove Shopping Center parking lot."

   C. We asked "for a teen center."

   D. "... nine teenagers had been arrested for fighting during the last month."

How do you think you did? Below, write down how many answers you think you've answered correctly.

I think I have answered ____ out of 4 questions correctly.

(Be sure to check your answers against those in the Answer Key, page 252. After the review, go over any areas that gave you problems.)

Short Essay Question for Fact versus Opinion

Is the statement "A meeting place for us kids is a great idea for our town" an example of **Fact** or **Opinion**? Please explain.

Pre-Writing Section
Use the space provided to make a writing plan for your essay.

Essay

Now that you have finished writing, use the **4 Essay Keys** to give your work a grade.

Short Essay Grading Key

1. Thoroughly answered the question being asked.	4	3	2	1	0
2. Used enough supporting details in the essay.	4	3	2	1	0
3. Covered the topic completely and with insight.	4	3	2	1	0
4. Used correct grammar, spelling, and vocabulary.	4	3	2	1	0

Overall Grade 4 3 2 1 0

Scoring

4 Outstanding essay
3 Above-average writing with few mistakes
2 Average writing with some mistakes, little use of text, simple or false reasoning, and a simple writing style
1 Below-average writing with many mistakes, unclear references, too much opinion, and many grammar, vocabulary, and spelling errors
0 Poorly written response that didn't relate to the question, answer it directly, or address the topic

(Be sure to check your answers against those in the Answer Key, page 253.)

Long Essay for Fact Versus Opinion

Victoria asks for a meeting place where she and her friends can go. She says, "If you (Mayor Patel) gave us a teen center, there wouldn't be any more trouble in town because we'd be off the streets. We'd all want to be with our friends." Is this an example of **Fact** or **Opinion**? Please explain in detail.

Pre-Writing Section

Use the space provided to make a writing plan for your essay.

Essay

Now that you have finished writing, use the **4 Essay Keys** to give your work a grade.

Long Essay Grading Key

1.	Thoroughly answered the question being asked.	4	3	2	1	0
2.	Used enough supporting details in the essay.	4	3	2	1	0
3.	Covered the topic completely and with insight.	4	3	2	1	0
4.	Used correct grammar, spelling, and vocabulary.	4	3	2	1	0

Overall Grade 4 3 2 1 0

Scoring

4 Outstanding essay
3 Above-average writing with few mistakes
2 Average writing with some mistakes, little use of text, simple or false reasoning, and a simple writing style
1 Below-average writing with many mistakes, unclear references, too much opinion, and many grammar, vocabulary, and spelling errors
0 Poorly written response that didn't relate to the question, answer it directly, or address the topic

(As you finish each section, be sure to check your answers with those in the Answer Key, page 253.)

TARGET SKILL 8: FOLLOWING DIRECTIONS

To do something well, we should make sure that we follow directions carefully. These are our guides for success.

STRATEGY

As you are doing your reading, use these strategies.

- Directions are given in order. We must follow the order to get the desired result.
  - Look for key words and phrases—for example, *First*, *Next*, and *After completing Step 1*.

- Look for warning phrases—for example, *Before continuing* and *Be sure to*.
- Only use the directions that are given to write your essay. Do not wander from the topic.

Practice

The passage that we'll read contains the guidelines to a Guided Book Report. The following questions deal with **Following Directions**.

Read the passage thoroughly to help to answer the questions. Answer the questions based on this passage by using the **PT**. Be sure to:

1. Preview the questions.
2. Preview the material.
3. Read the entire passage.

GUIDED READING BOOK REPORT—GUIDELINES

FREE CHOICE FICTION

Reading a good novel can be exciting. Finding out about the different characters and learning how the author blends each action and scene together are only some of the thrills you can have while reading. This experience can be a good one. If you read your book with a friend, you can discuss the book together. That means that it's OK to pick out a book to read with a friend, read the book together, and then discuss it too.
Once you select your book, you will need to follow these steps.

1. Find a friend who also wants to read the same book.
2. Have your parent/guardian sign your book permission slip.
3. Return your slip to Mr. Rhoades by February 26.
4. Write down the following information in your personal guided reading log:
   a. Your name.
   b. Your reading partner's name.
   c. The title and author of the book that you and your partner are reading.
5. Divide your book into three sections. Enter the page numbers into your reading log.

6. Write down the dates that you plan to meet to discuss each section of your book. Be sure to schedule a meeting at least once a week so you and your partner can complete the assignment no later than March 18.

You will be expected to finish reading the book and complete all the discussions with your partner. If you wish to read more quickly than the rest of the class, you may do so without worrying about discussing sections that you were not yet assigned to read. Sometimes when you are really interested in a book, you want to read ahead. This unit has been designed to encourage you to do that.

Once a week, you and your partner will form a guided reading small discussion group. You will meet for no more than 20 minutes with another pair of students who are reading a different book. One of you will serve as a group facilitator who will keep the discussion "on track." You will also select a recorder who will take notes that will be signed by all group members and submitted to Mr. Rhoades. Your group must answer the following questions each time you meet:

- What are the major events that have happened in this section of the novel?
- Who are the major characters, and what are their roles?
- What conflicts are occurring?
- What is the biggest change you have observed from the beginning to the end of the section?
- Who is your favorite character in this section and why?
- What advice would you give to the main characters at this stage of the book?
- What grade (A, B, etc.) would you give this section of the book and why?

When you finish your student meetings, you will then share your responses with Mr. Rhoades. You must complete all three sessions by the March 18 deadline stated to receive two "A+" grades. Completing two sessions will earn you two "C" grades. Completing one session will earn you two "D" grades. A failure to complete any sessions will result in two "0" grades.

If you have any questions during this unit, please ask Mr. Rhoades at once. Also, please share with Mr. Rhoades any difficulties and successes that you may have.

Practice Questions

Answer the questions based on this passage using our **PT**. Circle each correct answer.

1. What type of book is being assigned for the Guided Reading Book Report?

    A. Free Choice

    B. Free Choice Fiction

    C. Free Choice Non-fiction

    D. Free Choice Biography

2. What is the next step after "Have your parent/guardian sign your book permission slip"?

    A. Find a friend who also wants to read the same book.

    B. Ask a parent/guardian to help you to select a book.

    C. Have your partner sign your book permission slip.

    D. Return your book permission slip to Mr. Rhoades by February 26.

3. Which of the following information does **NOT** need to be included "in your personal guided reading log"?

    A. Your name

    B. Your reading partner's name

    C. Your parent/guardian's signature

    D. The title and author of the book that you and your partner are reading

4. Which of these grades will a student earn by completing two guided reading sessions?

    A. Two "A+" grades

    B. Two "C+" grades

    C. Two "C" grades

    D. Two "D" grades

How do you think you did? Write down how many answers you think you've answered correctly.

I think I have answered _____ out of 4 questions correctly.

(Be sure to check your answers against those in the Answer Key, page 253. After the review, go over any areas that gave you problems.)

Short Essay for Following Directions

Describe the steps needed to form a guided reading small discussion group. You do **not** need to discuss the questions that will be asked.

Pre-Writing Section

Use the space provided to make a writing plan for your essay.

Essay

Now that you have finished writing, use the **4 Essay Keys** to give your work a grade.

Short Essay Grading Key

1. Thoroughly answered the question being asked.   4   3   2   1   0
2. Used enough supporting details in the essay.   4   3   2   1   0
3. Covered the topic completely and with insight.   4   3   2   1   0
4. Used correct grammar, spelling, and vocabulary.   4   3   2   1   0

Overall Grade 4 3 2 1 0

Scoring

4   Outstanding essay
3   Above-average writing with few mistakes
2   Average writing with some mistakes, little use of text, simple or false reasoning, and a simple writing style
1   Below-average writing with many mistakes, unclear references, too much opinion, and many grammar, vocabulary, and spelling errors
0   Poorly written response that didn't relate to the question, answer it directly, or address the topic

(Be sure to check your answers against those in the Answer Key, page 254.)

Long Essay for Following Directions

What are the questions that the two pairs of students are required to share each time they meet? Please explain in detail.

Pre-Writing Section

Use the space provided to make a writing plan for your essay.

Essay

Now that you have finished writing, use the **4 Essay Keys** to give your work a grade.

Long Essay Grading Key

1. Thoroughly answered the question being asked.	4	3	2	1	0
2. Used enough supporting details in the essay.	4	3	2	1	0
3. Covered the topic completely and with insight.	4	3	2	1	0
4. Used correct grammar, spelling, and vocabulary.	4	3	2	1	0

Overall Grade 4 3 2 1 0

Scoring

4   Outstanding essay
3   Above-average writing with few mistakes
2   Average writing with some mistakes, little use of text, simple or false reasoning, and a simple writing style
1   Below-average writing with many mistakes, unclear references, too much opinion, and many grammar, vocabulary, and spelling errors
0   Poorly written response that didn't relate to the question, answer it directly, or address the topic

(As you finish each section, be sure to check your answers with those in the Answer Key, page 254.)

TARGET SKILL 9: RECOGNIZING LITERARY FORMS AND INFORMATION SOURCES

There are many types of literary forms, including novels, short stories, and poetry. There are also many information sources such as books, magazines, and Internet sites.

STRATEGY

As you read literature:

- Always look for the theme, the main character(s), the setting, and the conflict/resolution. These have been covered in the previous chapter.

As you read information sources:

■ Always look for the main idea and supporting details.

Practice

The passage that we'll read is typical of a 7th grader's work. The questions that follow deal with **Recognizing Literary Forms and Information Sources**.

Read the passage thoroughly to help to answer the questions. Answer the questions based on this passage by using the **PT**. **Be sure to**

> 1. Preview the questions.
> 2. Preview the material.
> 3. Read the entire passage.

PROFESSIONAL SPORTS BROADCASTING—MY DREAM JOB

by Philip Cheung

I've always wanted to be a professional sports broadcaster. That's all I've ever wanted to be. While my friends talk about their dreams of becoming movie stars, hip hop artists, fashion designers, or chefs, I just smile. While all of those career choices might be exciting, they don't get me personally excited. If the conversation happened to turn to sports broadcasting, however, then I would join right in and tell everybody about my plans.

You see, I've never wanted to do anything else. Becoming a professional sports broadcaster is my dream job. Whenever my friends and I would play ball, I would think about what it would be like to be sitting in a booth with the TV cameras pointed directly at me. I would talk about my team's record, our recent successes and failures, and our strategy for winning today's game. Then I would call over my friend Karl and interview him about the great catches he's been making all year. If there was time, I would interview a player from the opposing team to discuss their recent progress.

Most people might say that I wouldn't be able to play the game and announce it at the same time. I disagree. I plan to introduce a whole new way to broadcast a game. Sometimes the manager of a team is "hooked up" to a microphone during a game. I've even seen this done with certain star players. Why couldn't I do the same thing? I could describe the game and give my commentary right from the playing field. Who would be better to describe the game than somebody who's right in the middle of the game? Yes, that "somebody" would be me.

Now I know that I have to go to school "to learn my trade," as my dad is always telling me. That's not a problem. I'm willing to work hard to realize this dream. I won't give up until I make it.

I'm already reading a lot of books about famous sports broadcasters. Right now, I'm reading books about Mel Allen, Red Barber, Howard Cosell, Jon Miller, and Jim McKay. I've written a short story for my English class. It involves my meeting with Phil Rizzuto, the Hall of Fame player and former broadcaster. I've even written a song about becoming a sports broadcaster. It's called "My Search for Air Time." I played it during our school's talent show, and I won third place.

My favorite sports poem is "Casey at the Bat." The main character, Casey, had a lot of confidence. He probably had too much because he didn't even swing at the first two strikes. What a great interview I could have with Casey. I would run over to him and ask him about his decision not to swing at the first two pitches. I'd also ask him if he felt that he tried his best to hit the last pitch. Then I would probably have to stop the interview because Casey might be angry with me.

I'm only in seventh grade now, but it's not too early to start preparing for my dream career. I've already joined the school newspaper to help me with my writing skills. I've volunteered to be a helper at the broadcasts of our high school's soccer games, as long as I'm not playing a game myself that day. I've also called our local cable television station and asked if I could maybe have a tour of the studio. If I'm lucky and my dream comes true, maybe I'll be a famous broadcaster and some seventh graders will call my station to ask for a tour. I'll gladly show him or her around.

Practice Questions

Answer the questions based on this passage using our PT. Circle each correct answer.

1. What is the main idea of Philip's essay?

    A. Phil's struggles in seventh grade

    B. Phil's dream to be a professional sports manager

    C. Phil's dream to be a professional sports announcer

    D. Phil's dream to be a hip hop artist

2. Philip's piece deals directly with his own life. What type of essay would it be?

    A. Autobiographical

    B. Biographical

    C. Fictional

    D. Poetic

3. Which of these statements would most likely **NOT** be true about books that feature famous sportscasters?

   A. The books feature sportscasters who enjoy sports.

   B. The books feature sportscasters who have received training before they began to broadcast.

   C. The books feature sportscasters who enjoy working with people.

   D. The books feature sportscasters who never cared about playing the game.

4. If Philip's piece were to be published, in which type of publication would it most likely be found?

   A. a professional broadcasting magazine

   B. a school literary magazine

   C. a university literary magazine

   D. a national weekly sports magazine

How do you think you did? Below, write down how many answers you think you've answered correctly.

I think I have answered ____ out of 4 questions correctly.

(Be sure to check your answers against those in the Answer Key, page 254. After the review, go over any areas that gave you problems.)

Informational (Everyday) Reading ■ 161

Short Essay for Recognizing Literary Forms and Information Sources

Describe how this student's written work would be different if it were written as a short story.

Pre-Writing Section
Use the space provided to make a writing plan for your essay.

Essay

Informational (Everyday) Reading ▪ 163

Now that you have finished writing, use the **4 Essay Keys** to give your work a grade.

Short Essay Grading Key

1.	Thoroughly answered the question being asked.	4	3	2	1	0
2.	Used enough supporting details in the essay.	4	3	2	1	0
3.	Covered the topic completely and with insight.	4	3	2	1	0
4.	Used correct grammar, spelling, and vocabulary.	4	3	2	1	0

Overall Grade 4 3 2 1 0

Scoring

4   Outstanding essay
3   Above-average writing with few mistakes
2   Average writing with some mistakes, little use of text, simple or false reasoning, and a simple writing style
1   Below-average writing with many mistakes, unclear references, too much opinion, and many grammar, vocabulary, and spelling errors
0   Poorly written response that didn't relate to the question, answer it directly, or address the topic

(Be sure to check your answers against those in the Answer Key, page 255.)

Long Essay for Recognizing Literary Forms and Information Sources

What changes would occur if this student piece were written as a poem? Please explain in detail.

Pre-Writing Section
Use the space provided to make a writing plan for your essay.

Essay

Now that you have finished writing, use the **4 Essay Keys** to give your work a grade.

Long Essay Grading Key

1. Thoroughly answered the question being asked.	4	3	2	1	0
2. Used enough supporting details in the essay.	4	3	2	1	0
3. Covered the topic completely and with insight.	4	3	2	1	0
4. Used correct grammar, spelling, and vocabulary.	4	3	2	1	0

Overall Grade 4 3 2 1 0

Scoring

4   Outstanding essay
3   Above-average writing with few mistakes
2   Average writing with some mistakes, little use of text, simple or false reasoning, and a simple writing style
1   Below-average writing with many mistakes, unclear references, too much opinion, and many grammar, vocabulary, and spelling errors
0   Poorly written response that didn't relate to the question, answer it directly, or address the topic

(As you finish each section, be sure to check your answers with those in the Answer Key, page 255.)

TARGET SKILL 10: FINDING INFORMATION AND ANSWERING WITH PRIOR KNOWLEDGE

Whenever you are reading textbooks, magazines, or other information sources, the material that you may be learning is blended with the material that you already know. For example, the guidelines that you are given to write a science report are combined with your prior knowledge about writing effective reports.

STRATEGY

As you read:

- Always find the main idea(s).
- Follow all the directions that you are given.
- Use the knowledge that you know to make your efforts even more effective.

Practice

The passage that we'll read is typical of a 7th grader's work. The questions that follow deal with **finding information and answering with prior knowledge.**

Read the passage thoroughly to help to answer the questions. Answer the questions based on this passage by using the **PT**. Be sure to:

> 1. Preview the questions.
> 2. Preview the material.
> 3. Read the entire passage.

GUIDELINES FOR MAKING A CLASS PRESENTATION

by Miss Ostrovsky

Your major assignment for this marking period is a five-minute presentation to the class. You will select any of the major topics that we have covered in our class and then re-teach that material to the other students in our class. You will be graded for your coverage of the material, your use of media, your platform (presenting) skills, and your professionalism. Remember that your information and the way you present it are both important. You will be graded on both areas.

Let's look at each of the categories on which you will be graded.

Coverage of Material

- You must select a major concept from our unit dealing with verbs. Select one of the following main divisions.
    - Transitive Verbs
        — Direct Objects
        — Indirect Objects
    - Intransitive and Linking Verbs
        — Predicate Complements
            - Predicate Nouns (and pronouns)
            - Predicate Adjectives
    - Subject/Verb Agreement
        — Singular
        — Plural
    - Helping (Auxiliary) Verbs
        — Part of a Verb Phrase
        — Part of a Contraction
    - Verb Modifiers
        — Adverbs
        — Adverb Phrases
- You must provide the following information:
    - Definitions
    - Rules
    - Examples
    - Exceptions (if any)

Your Use of Media

- Choose at least two of the following media options.
    - Computer Slide Show
        — Laptop Computer
        — LCD Projector
    - Flip Chart and Easel
    - White Board
    - Posters

- Follow our Classroom Guidelines for Graphics.
  - Clarity
  - Legibility
  - Color
  - Size
  - Shapes
- Give your media a test run a day or more before you present the lesson.

Your Platform (Presenting) Skills

- Speak effectively.
  - Volume
  - Pace
  - Inflection
- Use some gestures appropriately.
- Stand up straight.
- Make good eye contact.

Your Professionalism

- Stay in control at all times.
- Don't laugh or act silly with your friends.

Practice Questions

Answer the questions based on this passage using our **PT**. Circle each correct answer.

1. Which of the following is **NOT** a major verb division for Miss Ostrovsky's class?

    A. Transitive Verbs

    B. Intransitive and Linking Verbs

    C. Helping (Auxiliary) Verbs

    D. Conjugating Verbs

2. Besides using a laptop computer and an LCD projector for a computer slide show, what other piece of equipment would be the most useful for the slide show?

   A. Audio Headset

   B. Movie Screen

   C. Spiral Notebook

   D. Chalk Eraser

3. What is the likely result for a student who chooses not to follow the "Classroom Guidelines for Graphics"?

   A. No one will notice because the information is the most important part of the presentation.

   B. Miss Ostrovsky will give the student one more chance to do better.

   C. The student will receive a lower grade.

   D. The student will receive a detention.

4. What would be the most unlikely reason for Miss Ostrovsky to assign this project?

   A. She just bought a new computer.

   B. She's punishing the students for misbehaving.

   C. She's going on maternity leave.

   D. She understands that teaching with media helps to improve learning.

How do you think you did? Below, write down how many answers you think you've answered correctly.

I think I have answered ____ out of 4 questions correctly.

(Be sure to check your answers against those in the Answer Key, page 255. After the review, go over any areas that gave you problems.)

Short Essay on Finding Information and Answering with Prior Knowledge

Explain why it's important for Miss Ostrovsky's students to "maintain (their) professionalism."

Pre-Writing Section

Use the space provided to make a writing plan for your essay.

Essay

Now that you have finished writing, use the **4 Essay Keys** to give your work a grade.

Short Essay Grading Key

1. Thoroughly answered the question being asked.	4	3	2	1	0
2. Used enough supporting details in the essay.	4	3	2	1	0
3. Covered the topic completely and with insight.	4	3	2	1	0
4. Used correct grammar, spelling, and vocabulary.	4	3	2	1	0

Overall Grade 4 3 2 1 0

Scoring

4 Outstanding essay
3 Above-average writing with few mistakes
2 Average writing with some mistakes, little use of text, simple or false reasoning, and a simple writing style
1 Below-average writing with many mistakes, unclear references, too much opinion, and many grammar, vocabulary, and spelling errors
0 Poorly written response that didn't relate to the question, answer it directly, or address the topic

(Be sure to check your answers against those in the Answer Key, page 256.)

Long Essay for Finding Information and Answering with Prior Knowledge

When Miss Ostrovsky's students give their lessons about verbs, they must provide four different types of information. Explain why this information is important.

Pre-Writing Section
Use the space provided to make a writing plan for your essay.

Essay

Informational (Everyday) Reading

Now that you have finished writing, use the **4 Essay Keys** to give your work a grade.

Long Essay Grading Key

1.	Thoroughly answered the question being asked.	4	3	2	1	0
2.	Used enough supporting details in the essay.	4	3	2	1	0
3.	Covered the topic completely and with insight.	4	3	2	1	0
4.	Used correct grammar, spelling, and vocabulary.	4	3	2	1	0

Overall Grade 4 3 2 1 0

Scoring

4 Outstanding essay
3 Above-average writing with few mistakes
2 Average writing with some mistakes, little use of text, simple or false reasoning, and a simple writing style
1 Below-average writing with many mistakes, unclear references, too much opinion, and many grammar, vocabulary, and spelling errors
0 Poorly written response that didn't relate to the question, answer it directly, or address the topic

(As you finish each section, be sure to check your answers with those in the Answer Key, page 256.)

Chapter 5

GRAMMAR GUIDE: USING GRAMMAR CORRECTLY IN YOUR WRITING

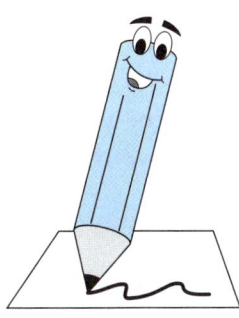

As we have already mentioned, the grammar that you use in your writing on the NJ ASK Grade 7 Language Arts Test must be correct. The score for your persuasive essay and your short and long essays uses grammar as one of the elements being graded. That's the reason why you must write sentences that do not have grammar mistakes.

When you write for any standardized test like the NJ ASK Grade 7 Language Arts Test, you always need to proofread your work. Checking the content of the essays that you write is important. It is also important to check your grammar.

Be sure to:

1. **Read each essay to yourself. Make sure that your sentences sound the right way.**
2. **Be sure that you have not broken any of the grammar rules that we are going to review together.**

Let's do some practice exercises so we can improve your chances of doing well on this test. Let's practice by concentrating on some of the most common areas that can cause you major problems with grammar.

TARGET SKILL 1: AGREEMENT—NUMBER, CASE, AND GENDER

There are three major points of agreement in your sentences.

1. Number—Singular or Plural
2. Case—Subject or Object
3. Gender—Masculine, Feminine, or Neutral

NUMBER

1. Make sure that your subjects agree in number with your verbs.
   a. When a noun is singular, the verb should also be singular.
   b. When a noun is plural, then the verb should also be plural.
   c. When there is more than one noun, then the verb is automatically plural.
2. Remember that singular verbs may end in "s" but plural verbs do not. This rule is the opposite of the one for nouns: "Use '-s' or '-es' at the end of many plural nouns."

Practice Exercise #1A

Read the following paragraph and then underline the three verbs that are incorrect. Write the correct form of the verb above the incorrect ones.

MY FRIEND AND I IS GOING TO THE VIDEO GAME STORE

After school today, my friend Sam and I don't plan to go straight home. Instead, we plan to go to the video game store. We is going to walk down Main Street and then turn right on Maple Avenue. There are three new games being released today, and we're going to be at the store to try them out.

(Be sure to check your answers with those in the Answer Key, page 257. After you review the answers, be sure to go back and review any areas that gave you problems.)

CASE

- Make sure that your sentences use the right case.
  1. There are two ways to use Subject Pronouns.
     a. Subject of the sentence; for example, "*I* am the President."
     b. Predicate Complement; for example, "The President is *I*."
  2. There are three ways to use Object Pronouns.
     a. Direct Object (answers "Whom" or "What" is receiving the action of the verb); for example, "Mom will take *me* to the skate park."
     b. Indirect Object (answers "To whom?" "To what?" "For whom?" or "For what?" the action of the verb is being done); for example, "Dad will make *us* dinner later."

c. Object of the Preposition (the noun or pronoun that ends the prepositional phrase); for example, "Give your ticket to *her*."

Practice Exercise #1B

Read the following paragraph and then underline the three pronouns that are used incorrectly. Write the correct form of the pronoun above the incorrect one.

OUR TEST REVIEW WAS A GAME!

Mr. Bogosian tried something new in class today: he played a review game to give we a chance to get ready for our test. Us kids actually had fun playing the game. Francisco answered the most questions so we clapped for he. Even so, we were the real winners since more than half of us earned our best test score of the year.

(Be sure to check your answers with those in the Answer Key, page 257. After you review the answers, be sure to go back and review any areas that gave you problems.)

GENDER

When your subjects are pronouns, make sure they agree in gender with your verbs.

1. Masculine (Male), Feminine (Female), and Neutral (neither Masculine nor Feminine) pronouns need the same gender for the nouns they are replacing.
   a. Masculine—Man ⇒ *He*, *Him*, and *His*
   b. Feminine—Female ⇒ *She*, *Her*, and *Hers*
   c. Neutral—neither Masculine nor Feminine ⇒ *It* and *Its*
2. Gender only matters with third person singular pronouns.

Practice Exercise #1C

For the following sentences, underline the correct answers.

1. Mrs. Cairo asked Mary to pick up (her, its) books.
2. Jackson took (his, its) brother to the movies.
3. The table can hold (her, its) own weight.

(Be sure to check your answers with those in the Answer Key, page 258. After you review the answers, be sure to go back and review any areas that gave you problems.)

TARGET SKILL 2: MISPLACED MODIFIERS

A misplaced modifier is simply one or more words that don't refer directly to the word(s) being modified. Instead, they refer to the wrong word(s). The result is confusion.

STRATEGY

1. Keep your word(s) next to or very close to the word(s) being modified.
2. If the meaning of your sentence is misleading, then rewrite it so it's clear.

Practice

Rewrite the following sentences correctly.

1. In her desk, Savannah found a blue lady's bracelet.

   _____

2. I once met a man with one arm named Rashawn.

   _____

3. I heard that the burglar has been captured on the evening news.

   _____

(Be sure to check your answers with those in the Answer Key, page 258. After you review the answers, be sure to go back and review any areas that gave you problems.)

TARGET SKILL 3: VOICE

There are two kinds of voice in all sentences.

1. Active Voice—The subject does the action in the sentence.
   Example: "The girls' twirling squad won the first place trophy in the county tournament."

2. **Passive Voice**—The subject does not do the action in the sentence.
   Example: "The first place trophy in the county tournament was won by the girls' twirling squad."

The active voice is preferred. Use it especially for standardized tests like the NJ ASK.

STRATEGY

1. Use the active voice to give your sentences a little more energy. Also, remember that the evaluators of standardized tests like the NJ ASK prefer the active voice.
2. Use the passive voice as little as you can on the NJ ASK.

Practice

Read the following sentences and rewrite them correctly in the active voice.

1. Every desk in the library was filled with students yesterday.

   _____

2. At my favorite ice cream store, my sundae was prepared by the new owner.

   _____

3. I was scolded by my parents when I didn't do all my chores yesterday.

   _____

(Be sure to check your answers with those in the Answer Key, page 258. After you review the answers, be sure to go back and review any areas that gave you problems.)

TARGET SKILL 4: SENTENCE VARIETY

When you write, your sentences should not follow the same pattern. Otherwise, they become very boring and difficult to read. The solution is to add variety when you write.

STRATEGY

1. Avoid starting every sentence with the subject and verb.
   a. Use a prepositional phrase or two to begin your sentence.
   Example: In the middle of the day, I usually eat my lunch.
   b. Use a prepositional phrase or two to end your sentence.
   Example: I usually eat my lunch in the middle of the day.
2. Combine two sentences to make a compound or complex sentence.
   a. Compound Sentence: Two sentences joined by adding a comma and the words "and," "or," or "but" to join the two sentences.
   Example: I went to the game, but my sister went to the park.
   b. Complex Sentence: A sentence that has one part that is a sentence and one that is not.
   Example: I went to the game while my sister went to the park.
3. Vary the length of each sentence.
   Example: I walked my dog yesterday. Because it was such a nice day, I went to my friend's house after I had my lunch.
4. Change the order of one or more adverbs, as long as the meaning stays the same.
   Example: Change "Tomorrow I will go home" to "I will go home tomorrow."

Practice

Read the following paragraph and then rewrite it so the sentences are varied.

GETTING IN TROUBLE

I got in trouble yesterday. My friends and I cut across our neighbor's lawn. He became very upset. He yelled at us. We said we weren't hurting anything. He said that somebody stole his lawn chair as a prank. Now he's blaming us. We're innocent. I guess we shouldn't have walked on his lawn.

_____

_____

_____

_____

_____

_____

_____

(Be sure to check your answers with those in the Answer Key, page 258. After you review the answers, be sure to go back and review any areas that gave you problems.)

TARGET SKILLS 5 AND 6: FRAGMENTS AND RUN-ONS

- A **fragment** is a piece of a sentence. It cannot stand alone as a sentence.
  Example: Hassan from the school around the corner.
- A **run-on** is more than one sentence that is joined incorrectly.
  Example: Francesca was bored she went to the movies.

STRATEGY

1. Change a fragment into a full sentence.
   Example: Hassan from the school around the corner is on my soccer team.
2. Here are two ways to fix a run-on.
   a. Separate the run-on into two different sentences.
      Example: Francesca was bored. Therefore, she went to the movies.
   b. Combine the run-on into one sentence.
      Example: Since Francesca was bored, she went to the movies.

Practice—Fragments

Rewrite the following sentences correctly to eliminate fragments.

1. Through the park.

_____

2. My best friend from Vineland.

   _____

3. Exercising every morning.

   _____

Practice—Run-ons

Rewrite the following sentences correctly to eliminate run-ons.

1. Come to my birthday party it will be fun.

   _____

2. I'm doing my homework now I can't talk to you

   _____

3. I'll take out the trash I'll walk the dog.

   _____

(Be sure to check your answers with those in the Answer Key, page 259. After you review the answers, be sure to go back and review any areas that gave you problems.)

TARGET SKILLS 7 AND 8: PUNCTUATION WITH COMMAS AND END MARKS

1. A **comma** has a few basic purposes in a sentence.
   a. It combines with the words "and," "or," or "but" to make a compound sentence.
      Example: I ran, but you walked.
   b. It separates more than two items in a series.
      Example: We ate, played games, and rode the rides at the amusement park.
   c. It's used when the first part of a complex sentence isn't a full sentence.
      Example: When we played video games, we had fun.
   d. It separates the name of a city from the name of a state.
      Example: Linden, New Jersey.

Grammar Guide: Using Grammar Correctly in Your Writing ▪ 187

      e. It's used after greetings and closings in letters.
          Example: "Dear Moira," and "Sincerely yours,"
      f. It's used after introductory words and phrases.
          Example: Yes, I'm coming now. **AND** During the winter, I like to ice skate.
      g. It's used with an appositive (a word that further explains another word).
          Example: My brother, a hard worker, was voted captain of the team.
2. There are four basic **end marks** used for sentences.
    a. Period
       i. Declarative Sentence (Statement).
          Example: I like ice cream.
      ii. Imperative Sentence (Command or Request).
          Example: Come here.
    b. Question Mark—Interrogative Sentence (Question).
       Example: Can you help me?
    c. Exclamation Mark—Exclamatory Sentence (Strong Feeling or Emotion).
       Example: We won the city championship!

STRATEGY

1. Learn the rules.
2. Follow the rules.

Practice—Commas

Punctuate the following sentences correctly by using commas correctly.

1. I had a hamburger and you had pizza.
2. My mom asked me to go to the store mail a letter and put my dirty clothes in the wash.
3. Because I earned all "A's" and "B's" on my report card I'm getting a reward.
4. We moved to New Jersey from Springfield Ohio.
5. "Sincerely yours Allen" is the ending I used for my letter.
6. No I won't make fun of the new student in our class.
7. The winner of the fund-raising challenge was Nicole a student from my class.

Practice—Punctuating Sentences

Punctuate the following sentences correctly.

1. I just won a million dollars
2. Please take care of yourself
3. Did you eat the last piece of cake
4. The class project will be due on March 3

(Be sure to check your answers with those in the Answer Key, page 260. After you review the answers, be sure to go back and review any areas that gave you problems.)

TARGET SKILLS 9 AND 10: HOMOPHONES AND HOMOGRAPHS

1. **Homophones** are words that sound alike and may be spelled alike or differently.
   Each set of homophones has the same pronunciation.
   Example: You can **pare** ("cut off") the limb of a **pear** ("fruit") tree. Then you can cut the limb into two equal pieces to make a **pair** ("set of two").
2. **Homographs** share the same spelling, but each has a different meaning.
   Example: The campers could not **bear** ("support") to think that a **bear** ("wild animal") might be wandering outside their tents.
3. **Homographs** may also have different pronunciations. For example, **"bow"** (to bend forward at the waist) and **"bow"** (the front of a ship) are pronounced differently than **"bow"** (a way to knot material like string and cloth).

STRATEGY

1. Make sure that you know the appropriate meaning of the homophones and homographs that you wish to use. Spelling and word choice do count on the NJ ASK.
2. For more examples of homophones and homographs, search the Internet.

Practice—Homophones

Underline the correct homophones in the following sentences.

1. I had to (so, sew) a button on my coat yesterday.
2. (Their, There, They're) not the same desserts that we had at the party last week.
3. Please hand in your homework (to, too, two) the teacher.
4. When you don't speak up, I can't (hear, here) you.
5. The petals on this lovely (flour, flower) have a pleasant aroma.

How do you think you did? Below, write down how many answers you think you have completed correctly.

I think I have answered _____ out of 5 questions correctly.

(Be sure to check your answers with those in the Answer Key, page 260. After you review the answers, be sure to go back and review any areas that gave you problems.)

Practice—Homographs

Choose the correct meaning of each homograph and write the correct letter after each sentence.

1. This tea was made from an exotic **bark**. ___
   a. an animal's cry
   b. the covering of a tree
2. My backpack was very **light** today. ___
   a. not heavy
   b. not dark
3. Of which local team are you a **fan**? ___
   a. admirer
   b. cooling device
4. Before you put on a bandage, be sure to clean your **wound**. ___
   a. turning in a circular way
   b. skin cut
5. Is this television program **live** or pre-recorded? ___
   a. residing in a place
   b. happening in the present time

How do you think you did? Below, write down how many answers you think you have completed correctly.

I think I have answered ____ out of 5 questions correctly.

(Be sure to check your answers with those in the Answer Key, page 261. After you review the answers, be sure to go back and review any areas that gave you problems.)

TARGET SKILL 11: GRAMMAR DEMONS

DEFINITION A—UNUSUAL ORDER

Some sentences have an unusual order.

1. **Inverted Order** sentences have their subjects placed after the verb.
    a. Some sentences that begin with **"Here"** or **"There."**
       Example: **Here** is the desk. **There** are the notebooks.
    b. Some declarative sentences are **Inverted Declaratives**.
       Example: In my classroom is my bag. Nearby are my shoes.

STRATEGY

1. Be sure that the subject and the verb agree in number in an **Inverted Order** sentence. As mentioned, look for the subject after the verb.
2. Use the same Strategy for **Inverted Declaratives**.

Practice—Unusual Order

Underline the correct verbs in the following sentences.

1. Here (is, are) four tickets to the movies.
2. Upstairs (is, are) your new outfit.
3. There (is, are) a rip in the carpet.
4. In the garage (is, are) your two baseball gloves.

How do you think you did? Below, write down how many answers you think you have completed correctly.

I think I have answered ____ out of 4 questions correctly.

(Be sure to check your answers with those in the Answer Key, page 261. After you review the answers, be sure to go back and review any areas that gave you problems.)

DEFINITION B—ADJECTIVE OR ADVERB

Adjectives and **Adverbs** are both modifiers.

1. **Adjectives** modify nouns and pronouns.
2. **Adverbs** modify verbs, adjectives, and other adverbs.

STRATEGY

1. Remember that many, but **not** all adverbs end in **"-ly."**
2. In the sentence **"You ran well,"** the word **"well"** is an adverb. You cannot use the word **"good,"** which is an adjective.
3. In the sentence **"You look well,"** the word **"well"** refers to health, but "You look good" refers to appearance.
4. When a verb is linking the subject with a predicate complement, the complement may be an adjective but never an adverb. Linking verbs are forms of "be" (*is*, *am*, *are*, *was*, and *were*) and the sensate verbs that refer to the five senses (sight, smell, taste, touch, and hear). These verbs include *looks*, *smells*, *tastes*, *feels*, and *sounds*. For example, say "The fish smells bad" because it has an odor. If you say "The fish smells badly," then you are saying that the fish doesn't sniff odors very well. Also, say "The music sounds loud" because "loudly" won't make sense (the music isn't making the sounds "loudly").

Practice

Underline the correct verbs in the following sentences.

1. That was a (good, well) meal.
2. Now that I have eaten, I feel (good, well).
3. I feel (bad, badly) about doing poorly on my science test.
4. The coach ended practice when we all performed (bad, badly).
5. I earned a (real, really) good grade on my English test.
6. My wish to be a singer someday is (real, really).

How do you think you did? Below, write down how many answers you think you have completed correctly.

I think I have answered ____ out of 6 questions correctly.

(Be sure to check your answers with those in the Answer Key, page 261. After you review the answers, be sure to go back and review any areas that gave you problems.)

DEFINITION C—QUOTATIONS

There are two types of **Quotations: Direct** and **Indirect**.

1. **Direct Quotations** contain the exact words that someone has said.
   Example: "Bring me the newspaper, please," said my uncle.
2. **Indirect Quotations** give the idea behind what someone has said, rather than the exact words.
   Example: My uncle asked me to bring the newspaper to him.

STRATEGY

1. Capitalize the first word of a **Direct Quotation**.
   Example: Mom asked, "Are you coming?"
2. Separate a quotation from the rest of the sentence by using a comma.
   Example: "I'm going to the video game store now," I said to my mom.
3. Do not use a comma to separate a quotation if there is an end punctuation mark (period, exclamation mark, or question mark) in the place where the comma would go.
   Example: "May I go to the video game store now?" I asked my mom.
4. For a divided quotation, don't start the second part with a capital letter unless it starts a sentence.
   Example: "Are you coming," Mom asked, "or are you staying home?"
   Example: "I'm not coming," I answered. "My report for health class is due tomorrow."
5. For quotations that have many sentences that follow one after the other, use one set of quotation marks only.
   Example: I told Kirsten, "Don't forget to bring the sunscreen to the beach. The last time we went, you forgot to bring the sunscreen. We don't want to get sunburned."
6. Periods go inside the closing quotation marks. Question marks and exclamation marks go outside the closing quotation marks **unless** the quotation is a question or an exclamation.
   Example: My brother said, "Let's go home."
   Example: My brother yelled, "Don't go in my room!"
   Example: Did Sarah really say, "I don't care"?

7. In a dialogue, start a new paragraph each time the speaker changes.
   Example: "Can you help me with my homework?" I asked my cousin Fred.
   "I'll be happy to help you," answered Fred.
   "If we finish early, we'll go to the mall," I said.
   "That's great!" Fred replied.

Practice—Quotations

Add the correct capital letters and punctuation marks to the following sentences.

1. The principal said over the intercom students, please report to the cafeteria at the end of second period today
2. Write your homework assignment in your notebooks said Mrs. Hudson
3. Are we there yet said my brother after every five minutes of our trip
4. Should we go to the park said Carrie or should we go to ball field
5. I answered we should go to the park they're having a special program there besides, all our friends will be there too
6. That's sounds great said Carrie

How do you think you did? Below, write down how many answers you think you have completed correctly.

I think I have answered ____ out of 6 questions correctly.

(Be sure to check your answers with those in the Answer Key, page 261. After you review the answers, be sure to go back and review any areas that gave you problems.)

DEFINITION D—UNDERLINING OR QUOTATION MARKS?

Titles of works are punctuated two ways.

1. **Underlining** is used for long works including books, newspapers, magazines, movies, plays, TV series, musical compositions, art works, and certain transportation (specific planes, trains, and spacecraft). Please note that italics can be used instead of underlining when you are typing.

Example: <u>The Pearl</u>, <u>The Star-Ledger</u>, *The Sound of Music*, and the *USS Missouri*.

2. **Quotation Marks** are used for short works including poems, short stories, articles, chapters of books, and songs.
   Example: "The Road Not Taken," "The Raven," and "Oh, Susannah."

STRATEGY

1. Use underlines for complete works that are long.
   Example: Last month, we read <u>Animal Farm</u> in our English class.
2. Use quotations for shorter works since they may actually be a part of a larger work.
   Example: We watched "The Confrontation," which is episode three of our favorite TV show.
3. Only use italics when you are typing on the computer. Do **NOT** try to write in italics.

Practice—Quotations

Add the correct underlines or quotes to the following sentences.

1. My sister is reading Great Expectations, a novel by Charles Dickens.
2. In class we read Dream Deferred, a poem by Langston Hughes.
3. Before the play-off game, we stood and took off our caps as the loudspeakers played God Bless America.
4. In class today, Mr. Porter read an article from The New York Times.

How do you think you did? Below, write down how many answers you think you have completed correctly.

I think I have answered _____ out of 4 questions correctly.

(Be sure to check your answers with those in the Answer Key, page 262. After you review the answers, be sure to go back and review any areas that gave you problems.)

TARGET SKILL 12: SPELLING DEMONS

DEFINITIONS

There are many **Spelling Demons** that we have trouble spelling correctly. Even adults struggle with these words.

STRATEGY

1. Learn how to spell correctly as many of these **Spelling Demons** as you possibly can. Remember, spelling and word choice count on the NJ ASK.
2. If you are unsure of the spelling of a word while you are taking the test, use a different word that you know how to spell correctly.
3. Go on the Internet and conduct a search for misspelled words. You'll find a number of lists that you can use to help you avoid these **Spelling Demons**.
4. Keep a personal spelling list. Write down any words that are difficult to spell. Check your list at least once a week to review these words.
5. Be sure to check the list in the **Appendix**. Feel free to add to this list as you find other **Spelling Demons**.

Practice—Homophones

Write the correct spelling above each misspelled word in the following sentences.

1. If you don't bring a note to excuse your abscence from school, you'll get a detention.
2. Let's buy some baloons for our party.
3. I am assigned the job of changing the date on the class calender.
4. The month after January is Febuary.
5. Do we have any grammer homework tonight?
6. Oops, my shoelaces are lose.
7. Our town's parade ocurred last weekend.

8. Mom asked me to get the butter for the mashed potatos.

9. Our music class is studying rythm and blues artists from the 1970's.

10. I used the vaccuum to pick up the dirt that spilled on the rug.

How do you think you did? Below, write down how many answers you think you have completed correctly.

I think I have answered _____ out of 10 questions correctly.

(Be sure to check your answers with those in the Answer Key, page 262. After you review the answers, be sure to go back and review any areas that gave you problems.)

Chapter 6

PRACTICE TEST 1: Answer Sheets

PART 1—WRITING

WRITING TASK A—PREWRITING SPACE
USE THE SPACE BELOW TO PLAN YOUR WRITING.

WRITING TASK A—PERSUASIVE LETTER

WRITING TASK B—PREWRITING SPACE
USE THE SPACE BELOW TO PLAN YOUR WRITING.

WRITING TASK B—SPECULATIVE ESSAY

PART II—READING NARRATIVE

MULTIPLE-CHOICE QUESTIONS

1. Ⓐ Ⓑ Ⓒ Ⓓ
2. Ⓐ Ⓑ Ⓒ Ⓓ
3. Ⓐ Ⓑ Ⓒ Ⓓ
4. Ⓐ Ⓑ Ⓒ Ⓓ

5. Ⓐ Ⓑ Ⓒ Ⓓ
6. Ⓐ Ⓑ Ⓒ Ⓓ
7. Ⓐ Ⓑ Ⓒ Ⓓ
8. Ⓐ Ⓑ Ⓒ Ⓓ

9. Ⓐ Ⓑ Ⓒ Ⓓ
10. Ⓐ Ⓑ Ⓒ Ⓓ

11. SHORT ESSAY

_____
_____
_____
_____
_____
_____
_____
_____
_____
_____
_____

©Copyright 2008 by Barron's Educational Series, Inc.

12. LONG ESSAY

12. LONG ESSAY (continued)

PART III—INFORMATIONAL READING

MULTIPLE-CHOICE QUESTIONS

1. Ⓐ Ⓑ Ⓒ Ⓓ
2. Ⓐ Ⓑ Ⓒ Ⓓ
3. Ⓐ Ⓑ Ⓒ Ⓓ
4. Ⓐ Ⓑ Ⓒ Ⓓ
5. Ⓐ Ⓑ Ⓒ Ⓓ
6. Ⓐ Ⓑ Ⓒ Ⓓ
7. Ⓐ Ⓑ Ⓒ Ⓓ
8. Ⓐ Ⓑ Ⓒ Ⓓ
9. Ⓐ Ⓑ Ⓒ Ⓓ
10. Ⓐ Ⓑ Ⓒ Ⓓ

11. SHORT ESSAY

___
___
___
___
___
___
___
___
___
___
___
___
___

12. LONG ESSAY

12. LONG ESSAY (continued)

PRACTICE TEST 1

PART I—WRITING

In this section, you'll be asked to write persuasively. Not every assignment on your actual test will require an essay. Many times, you are asked to write a persuasive letter. Be sure to use the correct friendly letter form when you write your letter.

WRITING TASK A—PERSUASIVE LETTER

Imagine that your school has been given the chance to participate in an experiment being conducted by the state department of education. Your school has been chosen to become an online school. All of your classes will be offered through the Internet. Classes will be offered right on the laptop computer that the school will provide for you. You will be expected to log on to your classes and spend a certain amount of time doing research on the Internet. Chat rooms, blogs, and e-mails will be common ways to communicate. You will never have to leave your home to attend a class.

Please write a letter to your principal and explain whether or not you think this idea is a good one. Make sure that you follow the proper guidelines for writing an effective persuasive piece. Before you begin writing your letter, do some pre-writing to organize your ideas.

Use the space provided on the answer sheets to plan your ideas before writing your letter. Then write your letter on the lines that follow.

WRITING TASK B—SPECULATIVE ESSAY

Imagine that you are visiting the amusement park and getting ready to board one of the exciting rides. You are at the park with either your brother or sister. Think about which exciting ride you might be getting ready to board. Now create a story and fill in the details of that story. Remember, your story should be based on events that most people would understand.

Do **not** simply describe what you see in your mind. Instead, make up a story about what is going on. You may wish to include some details that happened before your mental image took place.

Use the space proviced on the answer sheet to plan your ideas before writing your essay. Then write your essay on the lines that follow.

©Copyright 2008 by Barron's Educational Series, Inc.

PART II—READING NARRATIVE

In the following section, you will read a passage and answer the questions that follow. For each question, fill in the corresponding circle on the answer sheet. Read each question carefully and think about the answer.

THE ANT AND THE GRASSHOPPER

by Aesop

In a field one summer's day a Grasshopper was hopping about, chirping and singing to its heart's content. An Ant passed by, bearing along with great toil an ear of corn he was taking to the nest.

"Why not come and chat with me," said the Grasshopper, "instead of toiling and moiling in that way?"

"I am helping to lay up food for the winter," said the Ant, "and recommend you to do the same."

"Why bother about winter?" said the Grasshopper; we have plenty of food at present." But the Ant went on its way and continued its toil. When the winter came the Grasshopper had no food and found itself dying of hunger, while it saw the ants distributing every day corn and grain from the stores they had collected in the summer. Then the Grasshopper knew:

It is best to prepare for the days of necessity.

1. Which of these statements is **NOT** part of the plot?
   A. The Grasshopper was hopping in a field.
   B. The Grasshopper met the Ant.
   C. The Grasshopper helped the Ant.
   D. The Ant stored food for the winter.

2. Who are the characters in the poem?
   A. The Ant and the Grasshopper.
   B. The Ant and the other ants.
   C. The Grasshopper and the other ants.
   D. The Grasshopper, the Ant, and the other ants.

3. Which of the following is the main character in this fable?

   A. the Grasshopper

   B. the Ant

   C. the ants

   D. the farmer

4. In the beginning of the fable, where does the setting is take place?

   A. a field in the spring

   B. a field in the summer

   C. a field in the fall

   D. "A," "B," and "C"

5. During the summer, what did the ants store?

   A. bread

   B. milk

   C. corn

   D. hay

6. What season is it at the end of the fable?

   A. spring

   B. summer

   C. fall

   D. winter

7. Which of these would be the best theme for this fable?

   A. Always plan ahead.

   B. Cheaters never prosper.

   C. Take life one day at a time.

   D. Always tell the truth.

©Copyright 2008 by Barron's Educational Series, Inc.

8. What was the effect of the Grasshopper not listening to the Ant's advice?

   A. The Grasshopper lost its sight.

   B. The Grasshopper was dying of hunger.

   C. The Grasshopper declared war on the Ant.

   D. The Ant stored food for the winter.

9. In what physical condition was the Grasshopper at the end of this fable?

   A. was dying

   B. actually died

   C. made a full recovery

   D. moved to a warmer climate

10. From which point of view is this fable told?

    A. a first person narrator

    B. a second person narrator

    C. a third person narrator

    D. none of the above

11. Short Essay

Use the lines provided on the answer sheets to briefly explain the conflict in the fable and the way it is resolved.

12. Long Essay

Imagine that this fable was told from the Grasshopper's point of view. How would the story change? Would the Grasshopper present the details in the same way that the third person narrator has done? Explain your answer in detail. Use the lines provided on the answer sheet to write your essay.

PART III—INFORMATIONAL READING

In the following section, you will read a classroom handout and answer the questions that follow. For each question, fill in the corresponding circle on the answer sheet. Read each question carefully and think about the answer.

OAKVILLE MIDDLE SCHOOL 7TH GRADE FIELD TRIP INFO

Our annual Spring Field Trip has been scheduled for April 7. We'll be visiting the Elmore Kicks Soccer Stadium. Afterwards, we'll go to the Thrills Amusement Park in Delarton.

We will follow the normal procedures for turning in permission slips.

1. Permission slips will be sent out on March 17.
2. Signed permission slips must be returned no later than March 26. Only a parent or guardian may sign a slip.
3. Requests for group assignments will be accepted between March 27 and March 29.
4. Group assignments will be posted at lunch on April 6.

On the morning of April 7, we'll first report to homeroom for attendance and the flag salute. Second, we'll walk to the all-purpose meeting room to review our rules for behavior on our school field trips. Next, we'll review our agenda for the day. We'll also answer any questions that might arise. Finally, we'll distribute agendas for everyone to follow.

At 8:30 AM, we'll board our buses one homeroom at a time. Mrs. Moreno, our principal, will dismiss us. Our trip should take about 20 minutes so we expect to arrive at the Elmore Kicks Soccer Stadium at 9:00 AM. The stadium staff will each take a group on a tour of the facilities. We'll see how the field is maintained and how the athletes practice. Following the tour, we'll watch a skills demonstration performed by some of the Kicks' current team members. After the demonstration, our county Public School Soccer League champion Flyers will receive their trophies from Kicks President and former Oakdale MS student Rashad Crawford. Also, our Flyers will participate in a shootout with Kicks all-star goalie Sean Donnegal. Our visit will end with lunch generously provided by the Kicks.

At 11:45 AM, we'll board the buses to travel to Thrills Amusement Park. We expect to arrive by 12:15 PM. There'll be a number of educational programs for us. **We each must attend two programs and fill out our learning guides**. During any **free time**, you may ride any of the rides that are in operation. Because Thrills is not yet open for the season, all the rides will not be running. The Wild Water slides will be closed, but the Big Wheel Ferris wheel, the Spookville haunted house, the Airplane Flight Simulator, the Paratrooper ride that spins in the air, the spinning and twisting Tilt-a-Whirl, the Mountain Top roller coaster, the Steam Engine Choo Choo train ride, and the Skytram monorail will be operating.

©Copyright 2008 by Barron's Educational Series, Inc.

The schedule of the programs is as follows. The length of each program is in parentheses.

- 12:45 PM—How to Design an Exciting Amusement Park (30 minutes)
- 1:00 PM—Careers at an Amusement Park (30 minutes)
- 2:15 PM—Food Management, Preparation, and Sales—with Free Samples (45 minutes)
- 2:45 PM—How to Be an Amusement Park Character or Mascot (45 minutes)

At 5:00 PM, we'll meet at the main gate of Thrills. We'll board our buses and return to our school by 5:30 PM. Your parents and guardians should be prepared to pick you up at 5:30 PM.

1. On the morning of April 7, what will happen between "attendance and the flag salute" and the review of the day's agenda?
   A. Go to the all-purpose meeting room to review field trip behavior rules.
   B. Go back to homeroom for a question and answer session.
   C. Go to the cafeteria to wait for the buses.
   D. Go directly to the buses.

2. When will the agendas for the trip be handed out?
   A. before homeroom
   B. in homeroom
   C. in the all-purpose meeting room
   D. on the bus

3. After the tour of the Elmore Kicks Soccer Stadium, what is the next activity?
   A. the trophy presentation
   B. the shootout
   C. the skills demonstration
   D. lunch

4. If "Food Management, Preparation, and Sales—with Free Samples" is the first program a student attends, then which program must be the second program attended?
   A. How to Design an Exciting Amusement Park
   B. Careers at an Amusement Park
   C. Autographs and Photos with Kicks Players
   D. How to Be an Amusement Park Character or Mascot

5. During the field trip, which of the following is the most likely to happen to a student who wants to ride the water slide?

    A. The student will have a chance to win a prize.

    B. The student will be turned away.

    C. The student will have to meet a height and weight requirement.

    D. The student will probably have to wait in a long line.

6. Which of the following statements is a fact?

    A. The Oakville Middle School students will love this field trip.

    B. Some of the Oakville Middle School students will get in trouble at the park.

    C. The Oakville Middle School buses are expected to arrive at the Elmore Kicks Soccer Stadium at 9:00 AM.

    D. The students will not want to leave Thrills Amusement Park at the end of the day.

7. If this entire notice were made public, where is the most likely place it would be found?

    A. the Oakville Middle School Web site

    B. the Oakville community newspaper

    C. the local supermarket bulletin board

    D. the Elmore Kick's yearbook

8. When Thrills Amusement Park opens for the season, what will likely happen?

    A. There will be school field trips every day.

    B. The Wild Water Slides will be operating.

    C. The Airplane Flight Simulator will not be operating.

    D. The Elmore Kicks will play a game there.

9. Who is Rashad Crawford?

    A. Is the principal at Oakville Middle School.

    B. Is the Star Goalie of the Oakville Middle School Flyers.

    C. Is the Star Goalie of the Elmore Kicks.

    D. Is the president of the Elmore Kicks.

©Copyright 2008 by Barron's Educational Series, Inc.

10. What is the main point of this field trip notice?

　A. to entertain

　B. to punish

　C. to amuse

　D. to inform

11. Short Essay

Imagine that the Oakville Middle School Field Trip notice has been rewritten as a short story. Use the lines provided on the answer sheets to give three or four major changes that would need to be made.

12. Long Essay

Imagine that the Oakville Middle School Field Trip notice is written as a diary entry by one of the honor students. What changes should be made to make this diary an effective one? Use the lines provided on the answer sheet to write your essay.

Chapter 7

PRACTICE TEST 2: Answer Sheets

PART 1—WRITING

WRITING TASK A—PREWRITING SPACE
USE THE SPACE BELOW TO PLAN YOUR WRITING.

WRITING TASK A—PERSUASIVE LETTER

WRITING TASK B—PREWRITING SPACE
USE THE SPACE BELOW TO PLAN YOUR WRITING.

WRITING TASK B—SPECULATIVE ESSAY

PART II—READING NARRATIVE

MULTIPLE-CHOICE QUESTIONS

1. Ⓐ Ⓑ Ⓒ Ⓓ
2. Ⓐ Ⓑ Ⓒ Ⓓ
3. Ⓐ Ⓑ Ⓒ Ⓓ
4. Ⓐ Ⓑ Ⓒ Ⓓ
5. Ⓐ Ⓑ Ⓒ Ⓓ
6. Ⓐ Ⓑ Ⓒ Ⓓ
7. Ⓐ Ⓑ Ⓒ Ⓓ
8. Ⓐ Ⓑ Ⓒ Ⓓ
9. Ⓐ Ⓑ Ⓒ Ⓓ
10. Ⓐ Ⓑ Ⓒ Ⓓ

11. SHORT ESSAY

_____
_____
_____
_____
_____
_____
_____
_____
_____
_____
_____
_____
_____

12. LONG ESSAY

12. LONG ESSAY (continued)

PART III—INFORMATIONAL READING

MULTIPLE-CHOICE QUESTIONS

1. Ⓐ Ⓑ Ⓒ Ⓓ
2. Ⓐ Ⓑ Ⓒ Ⓓ
3. Ⓐ Ⓑ Ⓒ Ⓓ
4. Ⓐ Ⓑ Ⓒ Ⓓ

5. Ⓐ Ⓑ Ⓒ Ⓓ
6. Ⓐ Ⓑ Ⓒ Ⓓ
7. Ⓐ Ⓑ Ⓒ Ⓓ
8. Ⓐ Ⓑ Ⓒ Ⓓ

9. Ⓐ Ⓑ Ⓒ Ⓓ
10. Ⓐ Ⓑ Ⓒ Ⓓ

11. SHORT ESSAY

_____
_____
_____
_____
_____
_____
_____
_____
_____
_____
_____
_____
_____

12. LONG ESSAY

12. LONG ESSAY (continued)

PRACTICE TEST 2

PART 1—WRITING

In this section, you'll be asked to write persuasively. Not every assignment on your actual test will require a letter. Many times, you are asked to write a persuasive essay. Be sure to use the correct essay form when you write your essay.

WRITING TASK A—PERSUASIVE ESSAY

Some people feel that all public school students should wear uniforms. Do you agree or disagree? State your position and support it with three reasons. Give three supporting reasons to defend each reason.

Make sure that you follow the proper guidelines for writing an effective persuasive essay. Give your essay a title. Before you begin writing your essay, do some pre-writing to organize your ideas.

Use the space provided on the answer sheets to plan your ideas before writing your essay. Then write your essay on the lines that follow.

WRITING TASK B—SPECULATIVE ESSAY

Imagine that you are having an argument with someone who is the same age as you are. This other person can be a brother, sister, friend, neighbor, or even someone whom you don't know very well. Imagine what is happening in this picture. Now create a story and fill in the details of that story. Remember, your story should be based on events that most people would understand.

Do **not** simply describe what you see in your mind. Instead, make up a story about what is going on. You may wish to include some details that have happened before your mental image took place.

Use the space provided on the answer sheets to plan your ideas before writing your essay. Then write your essay on the lines that follow.

PART II—READING NARRATIVE

In the following section, you will read a poem and answer the questions that follow. For each question, fill in the corresponding circle on the answer sheet. Read each question carefully and think about the answer.

IF

by Rudyard Kipling

If you can keep your head when all about you
Are losing theirs and blaming it on you;
If you can trust yourself when all men doubt you,
But make allowance for their doubting too:
If you can wait and not be tired by waiting,
Or, being lied about, don't deal in lies,
Or being hated don't give way to hating,
And yet don't look too good, nor talk too wise;

If you can dream—and not make dreams your master;
If you can think—and not make thoughts your aim,
If you can meet with Triumph and Disaster
And treat those two impostors just the same:
If you can bear to hear the truth you've spoken
Twisted by knaves to make a trap for fools,
Or watch the things you gave your life to, broken,
And stoop and build 'em up with worn-out tools;

If you can make one heap of all your winnings
And risk it on one turn of pitch-and-toss,
And lose, and start again at your beginnings,
And never breathe a word about your loss:
If you can force your heart and nerve and sinew
To serve your turn long after they are gone,
And so hold on when there is nothing in you
Except the Will which says to them: "Hold on!"

If you can talk with crowds and keep your virtue,
Or walk with Kings—nor lose the common touch,
If neither foes nor loving friends can hurt you,
If all men count with you, but none too much:
If you can fill the unforgiving minute
With sixty seconds' worth of distance run,
Yours is the Earth and everything that's in it,
And—which is more—you'll be a Man, my son

1. What is the mood of the narrator in this poem?

   A. inspirational

   B. gloomy

   C. romantic

   D. confused

2. What is the tone of this poem?

   A. humorous

   B. serious

   C. happy

   D. sad

3. The phrase "If you can keep your head when all about you / Are losing theirs" is a metaphor. What does it mean?

   A. having your head not be cut off

   B. avoiding being deported from the country

   C. keeping all your money while others are not

   D. keeping calm

4. Why does Kipling say not to "look too good, nor talk too wise"?

   A. He values being sneaky.

   B. He values not looking good at another's expense.

   C. He values the freedom of being uneducated.

   D. He values his own good looks and intelligence.

5. What literary device is the line "If you can dream—and not make dreams your master" an example of?

   A. setting

   B. simile

   C. personification

   D. rhyme

6. The lines "If you can make one heap of all your winnings / And risk it on one turn of pitch-and-toss, / And lose, and start again at your beginnings, / And never breathe a word about your loss?" refer to which of the following?

   A. maturity

   B. defeat

   C. surrender

   D. confusion

7. In the first four lines of the second stanza "If you can dream—and not make dreams your master; / If you can think—and not make thoughts your aim, / If you can meet with Triumph and Disaster / And treat those two impostors just the same," which lines rhyme?

   A. lines 1 and 4

   B. lines 2 and 3

   C. lines 1 and 3 and lines 2 and 4

   D. lines 1, 2, and 3

8. The phrase "Twisted by knaves to make a trap for fools" is an example of what literary device?

   A. setting

   B. rhyme scheme

   C. simile

   D. alliteration

9. When Kipling says "If you can fill the unforgiving minute / With sixty seconds' worth of distance run," what advice is he giving?

   A. Rest as often as you can.

   B. Make the most of your time.

   C. Travel the world.

   D. Make many friends.

10. Which of the following would be the best alternate title for this poem?

   A. Never Take Chances

   B. Stay in School

   C. Important Advice for My Son

   D. A Plan for My Son to Be Rich

11. Short Essay

Use the lines provided on the answer sheets to briefly explain what Kipling means when he says in the first stanza, "If you can wait and not be tired by waiting, / Or, being lied about, don't deal in lies, / Or being hated don't give way to hating, / And yet don't look too good, nor talk too wise"?

12. Long Essay

How might the poem change if it were being written as a news story? Explain your answer in detail. Use the lines provided on the answer sheets to write your essay.

©Copyright 2008 by Barron's Educational Series, Inc.

PART III—INFORMATIONAL READING

In the following section, you will read a news article and answer the questions that follow. For each question, fill in the corresponding circle on the answer sheet. Read each question carefully and think about the answer.

A BRIEF HISTORY OF SKATEBOARDING

It is believed that skateboarding began in California. Sometime during the 1950's, California surfers began to "surf" on the streets with wheeled boards. The sport became very popular on the West Coast, but the popularity began to fade after a few years. When the popularity began to soar again, the sport began to spread across the United States. Today, it is a very popular sport among teenagers and young adults.

The 1900's

The first skateboards were made by kids. These looked like scooters with handles sticking out of a milk crate. Roller skate wheels are added to the base, usually a "two by four" piece of wood. The practice is limited to one of a neighborhood activity, not a sport.

The 1950's

Surfing becomes very popular in California. Skateboarding is "born" when California surfers decide to surf outside the water. The surfers fashion skateboards in the same way that kids have been doing. These surfers take small wooden boxes or pieces of wood and attach wheels from roller skates. Companies soon create laminated wood boards. Clay wheels begin to replace those made from steel, but the clay wheels break down quickly and don't have the proper grip. Skateboarding is first known as sidewalk surfing.

The 1960's

Makaha, Hobie, and other companies begin to stage competitions to raise the popularity of the sport. The sport becomes a fad like the hula hoop. Jan and Dean record "Sidewalk Surfin" in 1964.

Safety becomes an issue. Injuries are common. Communities begin to ban sidewalk surfing because of many safety issues. The popularity of the sport drops in the later part of the decade.

The 1970's

Clay wheels are replaced by urethane ones. With increased control, the boards are easier to ride on the sidewalk. Frank Nasworthy designs the smooth-running "Cadillac" wheel. The boards' decks increase in width, giving skaters more control and maneuverability.

The Zephyr team is impressive at the Ocean Festival in Del Mar, California. Zephyr's precision moves make sidewalk surfing a serious sport. Concrete skate parks become popular, skateboarders are ranked, and magazines and movies featuring skateboarding are increasing in number.

Skateboarders begin riding low to the ground. Maneuvers become more complex and difficult. The "Ollie" is credited to Alan "Ollie" Gelfand, who stomps his foot on his board's tail section, causes it to pop up in the air while he's riding. As skaters "take to the air," graphics appear on the undersides of the boards. Punk and new wave music are popular with skaters, and an anti-establishment attitude becomes common.

Skateboarding becomes less popular in the late '70's, especially when skateboarders perform on the walls of empty pools in California. With the amount and difficulty of tricks increasing, the number of accidents also increases. Many skate parks close due to high insurance costs.

The 1980's

The sport's popularity remains low in the early part of the decade. Contests are not as popular as they once were, contest prizes shrink, and sales of skateboards drop. Skateboard videos become popular. Stacey Peralta and George Powell form the Bones Brigade and make videos featuring skaters like Steve Caballero, Tony Hawk, Lance Mountain, and others.

As "the whole world" becomes "the place to perform," homemade ramps and handrails become popular places for skaters to do their moves. The moves become more freestyle, and vertical ("vert") skating is less popular than street skating in places like parking lots and roads.

The 1990's

In 1995, ESPN stages the first Extreme Games competition, helping the public to view skateboarding as a mainstream sport. In 1997, ESPN also holds the Winter X Games, including in-line skating and snowboarding.

Skateparks become popular in towns once again. The boards are more stable and easier to control, safety equipment is greatly improved thanks to modern technology, and corporations are taking an interest in the sport with skaters' clothing becoming popular in youth culture. The sport begins to move away from its underground style.

The 2000's (The Modern Era)

Skateboarding becomes even more mainstream. The decks of most boards are made from seven laminated sheets of Canadian maple wood. Wheels are hard so they slide better, allowing for greater speed and better maneuverability. Most professional skateboaders have corporate sponsors. Video skateboarding games are popular with young adults.

Skateboarding is spreading in popularity all over the world. In 2004, the "International Skateboarding Federation" is formed. The ISF begins serious discussion with the

International Olympic Committee. The ISF requests that skateboarding become a sanctioned Olympic sport.

Avril Lavigne records "Sk8er (Skater) Boi" in 2002.

In 2005, Danny Way sets a world record for skateboarding by jumping over the Great Wall of China without using a motor to boost him.

1. Which title is the best one for this passage?

   A. Sidewalk Surfing

   B. Skateboarding from the 1900's until the Present

   C. California Surfers Invent a New Sport That's Like Surfing

   D. Sidewalk Surfing for Kids

2. In the 1950's, California surfers make surfboards because ___.

   A. they are bored with surfing.

   B. surfing is outlawed after a tragic accident.

   C. they want to surf on land, too.

   D. they want to make a lot of money in competitions.

3. After the popularity of the sport rises in the first half of the 1960's, it ___.

   A. is even more popular though the rest of the decade.

   B. grows slowly in popularity.

   C. becomes popular with college athletes.

   D. drops in popularity as the decade ends.

4. In the 1970's, the result of the decks of the skateboards increase in width is ___.

   A. more control.

   B. better wheels.

   C. more popularity at the end of the decade.

   D. more skateparks being built in the late 1970's.

5. When it is said that skaters "take to the air" in the 1970's, it means ___.

   A. the skateboarders need a pilot's license to skate.

   B. the maneuvers are becoming aerial ones.

   C. skiiers are now becoming skaters, too.

   D. skateboarding is being covered on the radio: "on the air."

6. All of these statements appear in the paragraph about the 1980's **except** :

   A. The sport's popularity is low in the early part of the decade.

   B. Videos featuring skateboarding become popular.

   C. Skaters begin performing on homemade ramps and handrails.

   D. Allan "Ollie" Gelfand invents the "ollie."

7. Which of these statements about the 1980's is **NOT** an opinion?

   A. Skateboarding contests are not as popular as they should be.

   B. The sales of skateboards are too low.

   C. Freestyle moves are awesome.

   D. The Bones Brigade made videos.

8. The statement "In 1995, ESPN stages the first Extreme Games competition" is an example of

   A. opinion

   B. following directions

   C. making predictions

   D. fact

9. When preparing to write a report about the history of skateboarding, the best source to look for information is

   A. an encyclopedia

   B. fans of skateboarding

   C. a dictionary

   D. a novel about skateboarders

©Copyright 2008 by Barron's Educational Series, Inc.

10. What resource would be the least productive one to use to get information about skateboarding moves and techniques?

   A. professional skateboarders

   B. *Skateboarding* magazine

   C. skateboard repair manual

   D. skateboard shop owner

11. Short Essay

Explain two changes in skateboarding from the 1950's to the 1970's. Explain your answer by using details from the passage. Use the lines provided on the answer sheets to write your essay.

12. Long Essay

Explain the rise in popularity of skateboarding during the 1990's and 2000's. Use the lines provided on the answer sheets to write your essay.

Chapter 8

ANSWER KEYS AND EXPLANATIONS

CHAPTER 1

Suggested Sample Persuasive Essay Corrections

TITLE WE NEED HEALTHIER FOODS AND DRINKS AT MY SCHOOL (1)

If our school gave grades for the meals and drinks that many of us are (2) eating and drinking in school, would we get a lot of failing grades? It seems that many of us students aren't eating healthy lunches and snacks, and (3) these poor choices are harmful ones. Our general health and concentration is being affected negatively (4) . In addition (5), our families can't always provide us with the right nutritional choices. Therefore (6), we should eliminate the serving of unhealthy meals and snacks in our school.

By making better nutritional choices, we can increase our chances of focusing more directly on our lessons. Sugar and caffeine, which are common ingredients in many snack foods and drinks, have an adverse (7) effect (8) on our ability to maintain our concentration. We can pay attention in class and ask more thoughtful questions when we are not being distracted by the "rush" and the "slump" we get from these snacks. When we learn more, we can have a better chance to get higher scores on our quizzes, tests, and projects.

Eliminating unhealthy meals and snacks in school will help our bodies to develop (9) more properly. We should avoid foods and snacks that are not only high in sugar and caffeine, but also (10) in fats and salt. We need to stay strong to fight off and prevent various diseases like the common cold and the flu (11). We should try to stay healthy in our young years to battle (12) various diseases including high blood pressure, diabetes, bone diseases, and heart problems. The habits we establish now most likely will be the ones we will follow when we get older.

By making healthy food choices, we can also help our parents or guardians. Many of us live in "single parent" homes and homes in which our parents or guardians both work. We also have very busy schedules that we follow each day as we go to school, do our chores, play on teams, practice our musical instruments, "surf" the Internet **(13)**, play video games, listen to music, and spend time with our friends. Many of our schedules do not match with those of our parents or guardians. That is the reason **(14)** why we need help to make the correct nutritional choices, and our school can actually help us by making sure that our food and snacks are healthy ones.

By not eating the right foods and snacks in school, we are potentially causing ourselves a great deal of harm. We are hurting ourselves in the classroom by affecting our ability not only to concentrate, but also to do our best work. We are hurting our bodies by weakening our defenses **(15)** against everyday problems like colds and flu and more severe problems including diabetes and heart disease. We are hurting our parents' or guardians' **(16)** chances of helping us to be healthy since we are all following busy and hectic schedules that do not always allow us time to make the best food choices. We often choose the most convenient choices instead. I therefore believe that eliminating unhealthy meals and snacks in school is an idea that should be adopted today. Shouldn't we all strive **(17)** to receive a passing grade for our food choices as we grow up to be reasonable, intelligent, and healthy adults?

ESSAY KEY AND EXPLANATIONS

1. This change provides a more specific title that better fits the essay.
2. *Many of us* is a better choice since not all students are making poor choices. Also, we should change *food and snack* to *food and drink* choices.
3. Creating a compound sentence by combining the two sentences with a comma and the coordinating conjunction *and* adds sentence variety.
4. Adding the word *negatively* shows specifically the writer's position. Otherwise, the effect may actually be positive.
5. Never begin a sentence with *And*. It is too casual. Use a transition like *In addition*, *Moreover*, or *Also*.
6. Never begin a sentence with *So*. It is also too casual. Use a transition like *Consequently*, *Therefore*, or *As a result*.
7. The power word *adverse* is a better choice than the weaker word *bad*.
8. The word *effect* should be used here as a noun (a naming word), not a verb (a word showing action or state of being).
9. The word *develop* is commonly misspelled with an *e* at the end.
10. When you use the phrase *not only*, it is strongly suggested that you also use the phrase *but also*. Even so, try not to overuse this pairing by placing it no more than once in a paragraph.
11. The words *flu* and *flew* are common homophones that can be misused. Remember, *flu* is a medical condition and *flew* is the past tense form of *fly*.

12. The choice here is simple: just get to the point.
13. The word *Internet* is always capitalized.
14. The phrase *is why* is incorrect grammatically. You must say *is the reason why* instead.
15. The correct spelling is **defenses**.
16. For plurals that end in "-s" like the words *parents* and *guardians*, add an apostrophe at the end of each word: *parents'* and *guardians'*.
17. The power word *strive* is a better choice than the weaker word *try*.

INDEPENDENT WRITING PRACTICE PERSUASIVE ESSAY

Suggested Main Points

Possible points to support changing the standard ten-point grading scale.

- It is too easy to succeed under the present grading scale.
- Serious students would be rewarded for their efforts while less serious students would not receive the same rewards and considerations.
- Students will achieve higher levels of success because they will learn the value of hard work.
- Students who enroll in private schools that have a seven-point grading scale will not struggle since they will be used to working within that type of system.
- Students will not be as easily disappointed in high school when the requirements become more stringent and the workload increases.

Possible points to oppose the graduation requirement

- A seven-point grading scale leaves little room for a student to have a disappointing grade. One poor project or test grade can significantly lower a student's overall grade.
- Students should worry more about learning the material being studied rather than earning a high grade.
- Success isn't only measured in grades but in a system with a seven-point scale, the emphasis on grades becomes even more restrictive.
- Private schools and universities are looking for well-rounded students who are successful both inside and outside of the classroom.
- Success breeds more success. Sometimes it takes longer for some

©Copyright 2008 by Barron's Educational Series, Inc.

students to mature and be successful. Under a more restrictive system, they will feel more pressure and possibly give up before they learn how to succeed.

CHAPTER 2

SUGGESTED SAMPLE SPECULATIVE ESSAY CORRECTIONS

FRISKY SAVES THE DAY

As the sun came up, JJ looked at the alarm clock as she lay in bed. She had been asleep when she was woken up by the music from her clock radio and some other noise. The noise was coming from downstairs, and it seemed to be loud. She figured her mom would take care of it, but the noise kept going. How would JJ be able to sleep with all that noise?

JJ was known as being trustworthy. She always helped out people who needed help. She had stopped some kids at school from bullying another kid one time. She had taken care of a neighbor's dog while the neighbor was away. "I probably should help out in my house, too," she thought.

As she walked out of her room, she was able to tell that the noise that she had been hearing was coming from Frisky, her puppy. Frisky sounded excited, but JJ figured that her puppy was acting the way it always did. This puppy would run around non-stop for almost ten minutes at a time. The barking was probably just Frisky's way of being excited.

When JJ got downstairs, however, she noticed that it smelled as if something was burning. JJ called to her mom to ask if anything was wrong, but her mom didn't answer since she had just stepped outside for a moment. JJ called again, but still didn't get an answer. "Maybe something really is wrong," she said.

As JJ opened the door to the kitchen, the sun that would usually be in JJ's eyes was blocked since her mom had pulled down the shade. At once, JJ noticed that Frisky was barking and running around in circles. Before she could try to calm down her puppy, JJ noticed that there was smoke coming from the oven. JJ had to act quickly.

She started to fill up a bucket with water, but then JJ remembered a conversation she had last week with her Uncle Ralph.

JJ asked him, "Should you throw water on a fire?"

Her Uncle Ralph had replied, "Not if the fire is a grease fire—you know, like the ones in a kitchen. Then you should open a box of salt and throw the salt on the fire."

Luckily, the muffins hadn't caught fire yet. JJ was able to take a box of salt, look through the oven door to make sure the fire hadn't started yet, cautiously open the door, and remove the muffins before they caught fire. JJ turned off the oven as her mom raced into the kitchen.

"What happened, JJ?"

"Frisky's barking woke me up, and I came down just in time to turn off the oven and prevent a fire. Frisky's a hero, mom," JJ said with relief.

"You're a hero too, JJ. You may have saved our lives."

"Mom, please don't go outside again if the oven is on. It's dangerous."

"I promise," said JJ's mom.

Both JJ and her mom learned a valuable safety lesson that morning: never leave the stove or the oven unattended.

Notice that in this essay, the writer made the following improvements.

- The title relates directly to the main event in the story.

- There is more detailed description.
  - "As the sun came up, JJ looked at the alarm clock as she lay in bed."
  - "She had taken care of a neighbor's dog while the neighbor was away."

- The entire "scene" is painted completely.
  - "JJ was known as being trustworthy. She always helped out people who needed help. She had stopped some kids at school from bullying another kid one time. She had taken care of a neighbor's dog while the neighbor was away. 'I probably should help out in my house, too,' she thought."

- There is dialogue.
  - "What happened, JJ?"
  - "Frisky's barking woke me up, and I came down just in time to turn off the oven and prevent a fire. Frisky's a hero, mom," JJ said with relief.

- There are specifics.
  - The original sentence was "JJ was able to take a box of salt, make sure the fire hadn't started, open the door, and take out the muffins. JJ's mom raced into the kitchen."
  - It has been replaced by "JJ was able to take a box of salt, look through the oven door to make sure the fire hadn't started yet, cautiously open the door, and remove the muffins before they caught fire."

- There is a lesson that JJ and her mom both learn: "never leave the stove or the oven unattended."

This essay has now moved from the score of maybe "3" to a possible "5" or "6". There are more descriptive details in the revised version of the story. The new story is being told more completely. The dialogue helps the reader almost to hear the characters speaking. The specifics like JJ looking "through the oven door" and then "cautiously open(ing)" it make the scene more vivid. Finally, the

©Copyright 2008 by Barron's Educational Series, Inc.

addition of the lesson in the last paragraph brings the story to an effective closing.

INDEPENDENT WRITING PRACTICE SPECULATIVE ESSAY

Suggested Main Points

Possible information to include in your essay.

- The main conflict deals with the following problem: should the narrator Jean take the present and keep it, or should Jean try to find the person whose name is on the present?
- The plot (story line) deals with Jean walking down the street on the way to the store on Saturday morning around 10:00 AM. Jean turns a corner and sees the wrapped birthday present. There is no one around on this clear summer morning.
- The setting is a small town in the summer. There is no one on the street where Jean finds the present. In the town, most people know each other. However, even this fact doesn't help Jean to know for whom the present is intended since the name on the tag has been smeared by the moisture from the morning dew.
- Jean is an honest seventh grader who always tries to do the right thing. She is a member of the student council at school, and she has been a girl scout since she was eight years old. She also won the award for most reliable student at school last year when she was in sixth grade.
- Jean tries to find someone to ask for advice about whether or not she should try to find the owner of the present. She first meets Harriet from school, who advises Jean to keep the present. Jean's too honest and doesn't think that Harriet's advice is good.
- Jean's best friend Miriam comes by and tells her that Jean should follow the advice she always gives to Miriam: "Honesty is the best policy." Jean agrees with Miriam, and the two girls walk one block to the police station to turn in the present they have found.
- The working title for the story is "Jean Finds a Present." The final title is "Jean Takes Her Own Advice."

CHAPTER 3

TARGET SKILLS 1-3: PLOT, CHARACTER, AND SETTING

Practice Questions

1. The correct answer is **B. Uncle Henry always laughed**. Sentence #1 in paragraph #3 tells us **"Uncle Henry never laughed."** In

paragraph #1, we learned that "**A. Dorothy lived with her Uncle Henry and Aunt Em.**" In paragraph #5, "**C. Uncle Henry and Dorothy heard 'a low wail of the wind' that came from the south.**" In the last paragraph, "**D. Aunt Em warned Dorothy to go in the cellar to protect herself from the cyclone that was expected to arrive.**"

2. The event that is "out of sequence" is "**B. Aunt Em warned Dorothy to 'Run for the cellar!'**" It is in the last paragraph. Answer "**A. Dorothy saw 'nothing but the great gray prairie on every side of her**" is in paragraph #2. Answer "**C. Uncle Henry sat upon the doorstep and looked anxiously at the sky**" is in paragraph #4. Finally, answer "**D. Uncle Henry 'ran toward the shed where the cows and horses were kept'**" is in paragraph #6.

3. The story is set in "**D. The prairies in Kansas.**" Dorothy did originally come from "**A. An orphanage,**" but she lived there before arriving on the farm. Answer "**B. The mountains and prairies in Kansas**" is only partly correct since there are no mountains being mentioned. This is a **trick question**. Answer "**C. The eastern coast of the United States**" is wrong because Kansas is in the Midwest.

4. Answer "**A. He always laughs**" is correct because you are being asked to tell which answer is **Not** correct. If you read the question too quickly, you might have missed the word "**Not.**" Answers "**B. He works hard,**" "**C. His hair is gray,**" and "**D. He is serious**" can all be found in the third paragraph.

Short Essay—Sample #1

Dorothy lives on a farm. She lives with her Uncle Henry and Aunt Em. She grows corn because that's what they grow in Kansas. I know because I've been there. Dorothy's a happy orphan. She laughs and makes her Aunt Em "scream and press her hand upon her heart." That's spooky. Dorothy loves Toto, her little black dog who's not gray. Duh!

Explanation of Grade

The essay probably earns a "1" or possibly a "2" because it

- answers more than it's required to answer.
- doesn't always give accurate information about Dorothy.
- mentions growing corn, which is never mentioned in the story.
- says Aunt Em does "scream and press her hand upon her heart" when Dorothy laughs, but the reader's never told that Aunt Em's discomfort makes Dorothy happy.
- uses inappropriate "Duh" remark.

©Copyright 2008 by Barron's Educational Series, Inc.

- avoids spelling mistakes, but the vocabulary and sentence structure are simple.

Short Essay—Sample #2

Dorothy is an orphan girl who faces the challenge of living in dreary surroundings. Her Uncle Henry and Auntie Em, two people who are struggling to fight the drought that's hurting their farm, have adopted her. It's lucky that Dorothy has Toto to make her laugh because her Uncle Henry and Aunt Em are described as being "gray." That means that there is no joy in either their surroundings or their lives. Furthermore, the passage ends with Dorothy, Uncle Henry, and Aunt Em facing the prospect of a terrible cyclone hitting the farm. It's amazing that Dorothy can find a way to laugh while living in such a depressing place.

Explanation of Grade

This essay probably earns a "4" because it

- thoroughly explains Dorothy's character.
- notes that Dorothy is an orphan girl who faces the challenge of living in dreary surroundings.
- mentions the struggles Uncle Henry and Aunt Em face, along with the joy Toto brings to the "gray" individuals who have "no joy in either their surroundings or their lives" and the impending cyclone.
- uses insight by stating, "It's amazing that Dorothy can find a way to laugh while living in such a depressing place."
- Uses appropriate grammar, spelling, and vocabulary and sentence variety.

Long Essay—Sample #1

Life on Uncle Henry and Aunt Em's farm was not very pleasant. In the first paragraph, the author spoke of a small home with not much more than "four walls, a floor and a roof." The interior contained "a rusty looking cookstove, a cupboard for the dishes, a table, three or four chairs, and the beds," along with a cyclone center. Outside was "the great gray prairie," plowed land that had been baked "into a gray mass," and gray grass. In fact, even the grass and the house paint were "dull and grey." This is not a pleasant place in which to live.

Not only has the author L. Frank Baum used the gray and simple setting to make the farm a depressing place to be, but he has also made the adult characters dull. Aunt Em was once "a young, pretty wife" who has become a "thin and gaunt person who never smiled now." In fact, Aunt Em was "startled . . . whenever Dorothy's merry voice reached her ears." Uncle Henry was also someone who "worked hard from morning till night and did not know what joy was." Like Aunt Em, he "was gray also," he "looked stern and solemn," and he "rarely spoke."

Explanation of Grade

This essay probably earns a "4" because it

- uses good essay construction.
- adds examples of "how difficult it must be to live" on the farm.
- mentions the farm's physical traits and Uncle Henry and Aunt Em's personalities.
- adds insight by connecting the dullness of both the setting and the characters.
- uses a variety of sentence structure.
- uses grammar, vocabulary, and spelling accurately.

Long Essay—Sample #2

Life on Uncle Henry and Aunt Em's farm was the pits. It was terrible. Everything was gray. The house was to small. The ground was hard and dry. Dorothy was happy. Her uncle and aunt weren't. They need to watch some music videos to cheer them up. That's what I always do.

Explanation of Grade

This essay probably earns a "1" because it

- is poorly constructed.
- has little support information from the text.
- uses no direct quotes.
- has simple sentences.
- makes an inappropriate comment: Uncle Henry and Aunt Em "watch some music videos to cheer . . . up." There was no television at the time.
- contains one spelling mistake ("The house was to small" should be ". . . too small"), no major grammar mistakes, and average sentence structure.

TARGET SKILLS 4, 5, & 6: THEME, CAUSE AND EFFECT, AND POINT OF VIEW

Practice Questions

1. The correct answer is **"A. first person"** because the author uses "I" often. Answers **"B. second person"** and **"C. third person"** are not used when "I" is used. Answer **"D. none of the above"** is incorrect because the poem has to be told in one of the three persons mentioned.

©Copyright 2008 by Barron's Educational Series, Inc.

2. The correct answer is "D. The traveler was sad that he couldn't travel both roads." The sentence #2 in stanza #1 says that the traveler was "sorry I (he) could not travel both." Answers "A. The traveler was lost" and "B. The traveler was hungry" aren't mentioned in the poem. Answer "C. The traveler was happy that he could travel both roads" is the opposite of the correct answer (D).
3. The correct answer is "A. The traveler hoped but doubted he would take the other road some day." Answer "B. The traveler was sure he would take the other road some day" is disproved by answer "A." Answers "C. The traveler was paralyzed with fear" and "D. The traveler was encouraged by his friend to take the other road" don't appear in the poem.
4. The correct answer is "C. The choice of the road taken changes the traveler's life." Answer "B. The choice of the road taken is a challenge" is a possibility, but answer "C." is better because it's more accurate. Answers "A. The choice of the road taken is a challenge" and "D. The choice of the road taken frustrated the traveler" don't appear in the poem.

Short Essay

Key Content Elements for Answer

a. Frost regrets finding two roads that crisscrossed in "a yellow wood" and could not travel both.
b. Traveler stood as long as he could to look down one of the roads "as far as I (he) could."
c. Add thoughts about difficulty when you make a decision.

Long Essay

Key Content Elements for Answer

Give the main information from each stanza.

a. The first stanza shows the traveler's regret that he found two roads that crisscrossed in "a yellow wood" and couldn't travel both.
b. The second stanza shows that the traveler decided to take "the other" road because "it was grassy and wanted wear." This image is a symbol for the traveler choosing to travel a road that is less familiar to him.
c. In the third stanza, the traveler notes that he has "kept the first (road) for another day." Even so, he doubts that he "should ever come back" to that easier, more familiar road.

d. The fourth stanza mentions the traveler plans to tell this tale about choosing the road "less traveled by" most people. He takes the road that contains the bigger challenge, "and that has made all the (positive) difference" in his life.

TARGET SKILLS 7 & 8: CONFLICT/RESOLUTION AND MAKING PREDICTIONS

Practice Questions

1. The correct answer is "**A. the youngest (the dwarf).**" Answers "**B. second oldest**" and "**C. oldest**" are incorrect because they wanted to tear down the anthill, kill the ducks to "roast them," and "kill the bees so they could get their honey." Answer "**D. all of the above**" cannot be correct since it would have to include answers "**B.**" and "**C.**"
2. The correct answer is "**B. Find all the missing pearls or be turned into stone.**" Answer "**A. Find the first hundred pearls or be turned into stone**" sounds correct since the oldest brother **did not** find even 100 pearls. If you had read the fable too quickly, you might have made this mistake. Answers "**C. Find the dwarf or be turned into stone**" and "**D. Find the princess or be turned into stone**" are not accurate. Only those who were unable to complete the challenges were turned into stone.
3. The correct answer is "**D. accepted the challenge and failed, also getting turned into stone.**" Answers "**A. ran away**" and "**B. locked the old man in a prison and escaped with his brothers**" do not happen in the story. Answer "**C. accepted the challenge and succeeded**" is true only for the little dwarf.
4. The correct answer is "**D. they would help him later in the story.**" Answers "**A. they would attack him because he's a dwarf,**" "**B. they would pay him money,**" and "**C. they would run away because they're afraid of dwarfs**" have no basis in the story.

Short Essay

Key Content Elements for Answer

- Tell what the reason (cause) is that the older brothers had fallen into "a wasteful foolish way of living" when they had gone "into the world to seek their fortunes."
- State that they laughed at their brother, the simple dwarf, when he had gone out to find them because they believed he was "so young and simple."

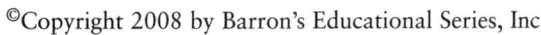
©Copyright 2008 by Barron's Educational Series, Inc.

- Mention that this fact helps to predict the irony that takes place when the younger brother's success occurs as a result of his earlier kindness.
- Cite at least one example from the text.

Long Essay

Key Content Elements for Answer

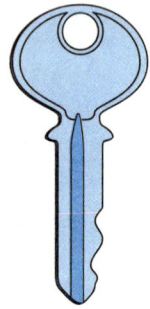

- The actions of the older brothers contrast with those of their younger brother, the dwarf.
- Neither of the two older brothers could find all the pearls since the task was too large for them. They were turned into stone when they failed.
- The dwarf managed because he had help. Unlike his brothers, he didn't seek conflict with the ants, the ducks, and the bees. The ants therefore helped him "to find the pearls," the ducks helped him to raise the "key of the princess's bed-chamber" from the bottom of the lake, and the queen bee helped to discover that the honey was only on the lips of "the youngest and the best of the king's three daughters."
- The resolution has irony: even though he was smaller in size, the dwarf's status and reputation grew to be larger than that of his two older brothers.

TARGET SKILLS 9 & 10: MOOD AND TONE

Practice Questions

1. The correct answer is "**D. gloomy.**" There are no signs of doom or despair. Answer "**A. formal**" is acceptable because the language is standard and polite, not slang. Answer "**B. clear**" is also acceptable, because the message is stated clearly. Answer "**C. realistic**" is acceptable since Longfellow speaks of "the Children's Hour," a chance to spend time with his children.
2. The correct answer is "**B. playful**" as noted in the children's "merry eyes" as they look to take Longfellow "by surprise." Answers "**A. nasty,**" "**C. angry,**" and "**D. sad**" are not typical emotions of children with "merry eyes."
3. The correct answer is "**D. challenging.**" Answer "**A. angry**" belies the poem's playful mood. Answer "**B. pompous**" is wrong since the poet is not arrogant. Answer "**C. sad**" is the opposite of the playful tone of this poem.
4. The correct answer is "**C. serious**" since Longfellow's words are similar to those in a news report. There's no evidence to support answers "**A. worried,**" "**B. sad,**" or "**D. humorous.**"

Short Essay

Key Content Elements for Answer

- The tone of the first three paragraphs is matter of fact. Longfellow hears "the patter of little feet" and "voices soft and sweet" as he anticipates spending time with his children during "Children's Hour."
- Longfellow anticipates the approach by "Grave Alice, and laughing Allegra, And Edith with golden hair" who are planning "To take me by surprise."

Long Essay

Key Content Elements for Answer

Include the playful nature that Longfellow feels. Mention that Longfellow is a very formal individual as the reader can tell by his phrasing throughout the poem. He says "Comes a pause in the day's occupations" instead of "Takes a break." He also uses a literary reference to a medieval folk tale entitled *The Mouse Tower of Bingen*.

Be sure to note that Longfellow seems to continue this pleasantly playful mood as he reports the advancement of his children who are "plotting and planning together" in an attempt to "surprise" him. The author uses a bit of irony as he refers to the youngsters as invaders who are looking to "enter my castle wall" to "devour me with kisses" and hugs ("Their arms about me entwine").

Longfellow completes the poem by playfully calling his children "banditti" (bandits) who shall be no match for "Such an old mustache as I am." He also includes a loving and respectful tone by promising to place his children "into the dungeon, In the round-tower of my heart." He wishes to hold these memories forever as he vows to keep the children near his heart "forever, Yes, forever and a day."

TARGET SKILLS 11-15: POETIC DEVICES: METAPHOR, SIMILE, PERSONIFICATION, RHYME SCHEME, AND ALLITERATION

Practice Questions

1. The correct answer is "**A. a tree.**" Answer "**B. grass**" is neither mentioned nor hinted at. Answer "**C. a mouth**" is part of the personified tree, and it's mentioned in line three and not line two. Answer "**D. robins**" is wrong because they lived in the tree. Also, they're mentioned in line eight, not line two.
2. The correct answer is "**C. get nourishment.**" Answers "**A. speak,**" "**B. cry,**" and "**D. yawn**" are incorrect because they're never mentioned.

©Copyright 2008 by Barron's Educational Series, Inc.

3. The correct answer is "D. all of the above" because the tree is compared to a person with arms (metaphor and personification). Also, the "l" sound is repeated in the words "lifts" and "leafy."
4. The correct answer is "D. both A. (metaphor) and C. (personification)." Answers "A. metaphor" and "C. personification" are incorrect unless they're combined. Answer "B. simile" is incorrect because there's no comparison using "like" or "as."

Short Essay

Key Content Elements for Answer

- The tree is compared to a person (personification).
- In the summer, the "nest of robins" is similar to a fancy comb or hair decoration being worn by a lady (metaphor).

Long Essay

Key Content Elements for Answer

- The extended metaphor personifies the tree as a person.
- The personified tree uses its "hungry mouth" instead of using its roots to feed.
- Like a devout person, the tree "lifts her leafy arms to pray," and the tree decorates "her hair" with "A nest of robins."
- This playful image is supported by the rhyme scheme that uses rhymed couplets (every two consecutive lines rhyme).
- The quote "only God can make a tree" is similar to the belief that only God can create a person.

CHAPTER 4

TARGET SKILLS 1 & 2: DETAILS AND SEQUENCE OF EVENTS

Practice Questions

1. The correct answer is "D. All events are listed in sequence" because answers "A. First, Jonathan 'had quickly written a note in his planner as he sat down at his desk,'" "B. Second, Jonathan 'was assigned to cover the school's wrestling matches,'" and "C. Third, Jonathan 'had received the highest grade in the class on the last test'" are following the correct sequence.

Answer Keys and Explanations ▪ 249

2. The correct answer is "**A. none.**" Answers "**B. one,**" "**C. two,**" and "**D. five**" do not appear in the text.

3. The correct answer is "**B. He thought his friends wouldn't think he was 'cool.'**" Answer "**A. His best friend had been thrown off the team**" is not mentioned in the text. Answers "**C. He thought Katie wouldn't think he was 'cool'**" and "**D. He thought his teachers wouldn't think he was 'cool'**" are proven wrong.

4. The correct answer is "**D. the school newspaper.**" Answers "**A. principal's newsletter**" and "**B. the parent-teacher's group's newsletter**" are wrong because he writes for a newspaper, not a newsletter. Don't be fooled by Answer "**C. the class newspaper.**" Even though Miss Rumson supported Jonathan, there is no mention of a class newspaper.

Short Essay

Key Content Elements for Answer

Your answer should include the fact that Jonathan had met Miss Rumson "when he was in central detention with her last year." Add that she had looked at some of his writing and enjoyed it. In fact, mention that she "even laughed at his story about falling off his bike while showing off to his friends." Conclude with a statement about his relationship with Miss Rumson giving him a positive start for the year.

Long Essay

Key Content Elements for Answer

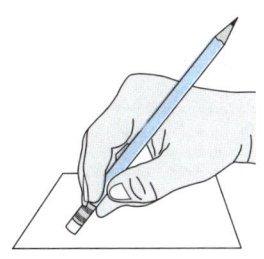

You should mention that things in school "really began to change for Jonathan" after he had joined the school newspaper. Point out that when he began to study, "he received the second highest grade on Miss Rumson's test." Mention that the head cheerleader "Katie asked him if he would study with her for the next test." Explain that his friends didn't tease him for being on the school newspaper because the "older brother of one of his friends was on the team." Add that Miss Rumson had called Jonathan's mom to tell her "that he had received the highest grade in the class on the last test" and that she had recommended him to the editor of the local newspaper. Be sure to conclude by stating that through hard work, things in school indeed "really began to change for Jonathan."

©Copyright 2008 by Barron's Educational Series, Inc.

TARGET SKILL 3: CENTRAL IDEA OR THEME

Practice Questions

1. The correct answer is "C. New Jersey Vacations for New Jersey Residents" since it reflects the **central idea or theme**." Answers "A. My Vacation," "B. Where to Take a Vacation," and "D. Vacations for All Seasons" are incorrect because none of them mentions New Jersey.
2. The correct answer is "B. The New Jersey seashore has swimming, shopping, food, and more." Answer "A. It's hot at the seashore" is wrong because it's not the main point. Answer "C. All of the historic areas are located at the New Jersey seashore" is not true. Answer "D. The New Jersey seashore doesn't get many visitors in the winter" is not mentioned anywhere in the passage and is not a main point.
3. The correct answer is "C. There are swimming pools in many towns" because it is not included in the paragraph. Answers A. "The Meadowlands Complex is the home of various professional sports teams," "B. There are eight different professional league parks for baseball" and "D. There are auto racetracks that sponsor NASCAR and NHRA races" are mentioned in the paragraph.
4. The correct answer is "A. The NJ Vietnam Veterans' Memorial is located near the Garden State Parkway." Answers "B. The Edison National Historic Site is located in West Orange," "C. The Fosterfields Living History Farm is located in Morris Plains," and "D. The C. A. Nothnagle Log House is located in Gibbstown" are all included as supporting details in the paragraph.

Short Essay

Key Content Elements for Answer

Your answer should include the fact that the mountains are a good place to vacation. You should add that both the Delaware Water Gap and the Skylands offer many activities including "skiing, snowboarding, and sledding."

Long Essay

Key Content Elements for Answer

You should mention that as someone who lives in New Jersey, "you could take a vacation without leaving our state." Be sure that you include the mountains, the seashore,

Answer Keys and Explanations 251

and the areas of sports and history" as vacation options. Also, mention some of the activities and places of interest in these areas.

Target Skills 4, 5, & 6: Questioning, Clarifying, and Predicting

Practice Questions

1. The correct answer is "**C. Upset because there would be less freedom in school.**" This information contrasts the sentence "Since school had let out last June, I suddenly had a lot more freedom." Answer "**A. Happy because the summer was boring**" is incorrect because Pat was enjoying the summer. There is no evidence to support answer "**B. Afraid because the school was in a different town.**" Answer "**D. Excited to be with friends again**" is wrong since Pat hung out with friends during the summer.

2. The correct answer is "**A. Pat's mom would be right**" since a mom's advice is usually good advice. Besides, Pat's mom was already making sure that Pat made it to school on time. Answer "**B. Pat would be right**" is incorrect because Pat is thinking about how much fun summer has been rather than how important it is to get ready for school. Answer "**C. Pat's brother would be right**" is not right because no mention is made of a brother. Answer "**D. All of the above**" is wrong, especially because it is disproved by Answer "**C. Pat's brother would be right.**"

3. The correct answer is "**D. all of the above.**" Answers "**A. Pat's new clothes might be ruined,**" "**B. Pat might get hurt and miss the first day of school,**" and "**D. Pat might miss the bus**" are concerns for Pat's mom. Remember, Pat's mom wakes Pat early because being late isn't "**the way you (Pat) want to start out your school year, is it?**"

4. The correct answer is "**C. eat a good breakfast**" because Pat was hungry around 10 AM on the first day of school and "Lunch wasn't on my (Pat's) schedule until noon." Answer "**B. sleep late**" is wrong because Pat won't sleep late until the weekend. Answer "**A. eat breakfast while wearing pajamas and sitting in front of the television**" was possible only during the summer. Answer "**D. walk the dog**" is wrong because there is no mention of a dog in the entire essay.

Short Essay

Key Content Elements for Answer

- Pat would probably sleep late.

©Copyright 2008 by Barron's Educational Series, Inc.

- Pat was used to staying in pajamas after waking up in the summer.
- Pat usually "made some cereal, poured a glass of juice, and settled in with my (Pat's) favorite television program on one of the music channels."
- Pat liked to "sleep a little later, eat lunch whenever I wanted to, watch my favorite daytime television programs, and just hang out with my friends," as well as skateboard.

Long Essay

Key Content Elements for Answer

- Pat's year will probably be a good one.
- Pat's mother cares because she wakes Pat up before the alarm rings. She reminds Pat to "Hurry up!" and not be late for the first day of school. She also says that being late would not be the way "to start out your(Pat's) school year."
- Having a caring parent or guardian is helpful for any student, especially one who doesn't eat enough breakfast on the first day of school.
- Pat seems to enjoy some classes and teachers.
- The only textbooks Pat has to carry home are for "math and public speaking."
- Pat thinks that social studies teacher "Mr. Barns is a great guy."
- "Gym was great because I (Pat) got to blow off a little steam."

Target Skill 7: Fact versus Opinion

Practice Questions

1. The correct answer is "A. Victoria Martinez wrote the letter to Mayor Patel." Answer "B. Victoria Martinez wrote the letter to her friends" is incorrect because Victoria talked about her friends but she didn't write them a letter. Answers "C. Mayor Patel wrote the letter to Victoria Martinez and her friends" and "D. Mayor Patel wrote the letter to Victoria Martinez" are wrong because Victoria wrote the letter.
2. The correct answer is "A. I believe that we should have a place in town. . . ." The word believe is an opinion word. Answers "B. . . . the building is closed," "C. Mr. Ross used to volunteer his time on the weekends," and "D. Mr. Ross retired and moved to Florida" are all facts that can be proven.
3. The correct answer is "C. . . . we go to the movies." Answers "A. The security guards are always chasing us away" and "B. . . . the security guards are mean to us" are Victoria's

opinions. Answer "D. . . . large groups of teens cause trouble" is not always true and is therefore an opinion.

4. The correct answer is "B. . . . there were too many kids hanging out in the Maple Grove Shopping Center parking lot." Answers "A. . . . we came to a town council meeting," "C. We asked for a teen center," and "D. . . . nine teenagers had been arrested for fighting during the last month" are all facts that can be proven.

Short Essay

Key Content Elements for Answer

- Victoria's statement is an opinion.
- Even if a meeting place would be a "great idea for our town," the word "great" makes this statement an opinion.
- Eliminating the word "great" would make the statement a fact.

Long Essay

Key Content Elements for Answer

- Victoria is giving an opinion.
- Her promise that "there wouldn't be any more trouble in town" can't be guaranteed because she doesn't control the behavior of all the teens in town.
- Her statement that "we'd be off the streets" is an opinion for the same reason.
- Victoria's statement that she and the teens in town would "all want to be with our friends" is her perception rather than fact.

Target Skill 8: Following Directions

1. The correct answer is "B. Free Choice Fiction." Answer "A. Free Choice" is incorrect because the word "Fiction" is not included. Answers "C. Free Choice Non-fiction" and "D. Free Choice Biography" are wrong. Even though they contain the phrase "Free Choice," the genres (types) are wrong.
2. The correct answer is "D. Return your book permission slip to Mr. Rhoades by February 26." Answer "A. Find a friend who also wants to read the same book" is wrong because it is the step before, not after, the second one. Answers "B. Ask a parent/guardian to help you to select a book" and "C. Have your partner sign your book permission slip" are not part of the list of steps.

©Copyright 2008 by Barron's Educational Series, Inc.

3. The correct answer is "**C. your parent/guardian's signature.**" Answers "**A. your name,**" "**B. your reading partner's name,**" and "**D. the title and author of the book that you and your partner are reading**" all need to be included in the reading log.
4. The correct answer is "**C. two 'C' grades.**" Answer "**A. two 'A+' grades**" is assigned for the completion of all three sections, not two. Answer "**B. two 'C+' grades**" is not a grade option. Answer "**D. two 'D' grades**" is assigned if only one section is completed.

Short Essay

Key Content Elements for Answer

- The student and his/her partner meet "for no more than 20 minutes with another pair of students who are reading a different book."
- One student "will serve as a group facilitator who will keep the discussion 'on track.'"
- A recorder will also be chosen to "take notes that will be signed by all group members and submitted to Mr. Rhoades."

Long Essay

Key Content Elements for Answer

- The students must discuss "the major events" in the section of the novel being discussed, along with the "conflicts," "the major characters," and "their roles."
- The discussion must include the "biggest change . . . from the beginning to the end of the section" and the reason for choosing a character as "your favorite," along with advice for "the main characters at this stage of the book."

Target Skill 9: Recognizing Literary Forms and Information Sources

1. The correct answer is "**C. Phil's dream to be a professional sports announcer.**" Answers "**A. Free Choice**" is incorrect because the word "**Fiction**" is not included. Answers "**C. Free Choice Non-fiction**" and "**D. Free Choice Biography**" are wrong. Even though they contain the phrase "**Free Choice,**" the genres (types) are wrong.
2. The correct answer is "**A. Autobiographical**" because it is written by Philip about himself. Answer "**B. Biographical**" is incorrect because someone else didn't write about Philip's life. Answer "**C. Fictional**" is incorrect because the information is

factual. Answer **"D. Poetic"** is wrong because the structure does not follow poetic structure.

3. The correct answer is **"D. The sportscasters never cared about playing the game."** Answers **"A. The sportscasters enjoy sports," "B. The sportscasters received training before they began to broadcast,"** and **"C. The sportscasters enjoy working with people"** are all traits of successful sportscasters.

4. The correct answer is **"B. A school literary magazine."** Answer **"A. A professional broadcasting magazine"** is not possible since the piece would not have enough interest for a professional audience. Answer **"C. A university literary magazine"** is not the place a seventh grader's essay would be published. Answer **"D. A national weekly sports magazine"** is wrong for the same reason.

Short Essay

Key Content Elements for Answer

- A short story could be fictional, but that is an option.
- There needs to be at least one main character who is facing a conflict.
- This conflict needs to be resolved.
- There will be a theme (main idea), which may actually teach a lesson.

Long Essay

Key Content Elements for Answer

- Paragraphs would be changed to stanzas.
- After each stanza, a line would be skipped before the next one would begin.
- A rhyme might be at the end of each line, but rhymes are not necessary in all modern poetry.
- Conversation or the main character's thoughts might appear.
- Sound and description would be more important in a poem than they would be in the original piece.

Target Skill 10: Finding Information and Answering with Prior Knowledge

1. The correct answer is **"D. conjugating verbs"** since it was not included in the list. Answers **"A. transitive verbs," "B. intransitive and linking verbs,"** and **"C. helping (auxiliary) verbs"** are all part of the list.

©Copyright 2008 by Barron's Educational Series, Inc.

2. The correct answer is "B. movie screen" because slides are shown on a screen. It is written by Philip about himself. Answer "A. audio headset" is incorrect because it is not necessary. Answers "C. spiral notebook" and "D. chalk eraser" are wrong because they have no direct use for a computer slide show.

3. The correct answer is "C. The student will receive a lower grade." Answer A. "No one will notice since the information is the most important part of the presentation" is wrong since Miss Ostrovsky has said that "your information and the way you present it are both important." There is neither evidence nor prior knowledge to lead one to conclude that answers "B. Miss Ostrovsky will give the student one more chance to do better" and "D. The student will receive a detention" are anything but incorrect.

4. The correct answer is "D. She understands that teaching with media helps to improve learning." Answer "A. She just bought a new computer" is wrong because the entire class could not complete their projects by using only Miss Ostrovsky's computer. Answer "B. She's punishing the students for misbehaving" is incorrect because this lesson is designed to help the students with their learning. Answer "C. She's going on maternity leave" is wrong because there is no connection between the assignment and a maternity leave.

Short Essay—Key Content Elements for Answer

- It's important for the students to "Stay in control at all times" when they are teaching their lessons because good teachers need to be in control of their classes.
- They should know their material well because this will help them to stay in control.
- The students should not "laugh or act silly with their friends."
- This type of behavior is rude and will only lead to more distractions.

Long Essay—Key Content Elements for Answer

- The definitions of the verb concepts being covered will give the students the basic information they will need to understand the concepts.
- The rules will help the students to learn the right way to use the concepts.
- The use of examples will provide the students with the chance to practice the concepts.
- Looking at exceptions will help the students to avoid making mistakes in the future.

CHAPTER 5

TARGET SKILL 1: AGREEMENT—NUMBER, CASE, AND GENDER

Answers—Exercise #1A—Number

1. Are
My Friend and I <u>Is</u> Going to the Video Game Store

After school today, my friend Sam and I don't plan to go straight home.
    2. plan   *3. are*
Instead, we <u>plans</u> to go to the video game store. We <u>is</u> going to walk down Main Street and then turn right on Maple Avenue. There are three new games being released today, and we're going to be at the store to try them out.

Explanations of Answers

1. The subject **"My friend and I"** is plural so the verb must also be plural: **"Are"**
2. The subject **"we"** is plural so the verb must also be plural: **"plan"**
3. Again, the subject **"we"** is plural so the verb must also be plural: **"are"**

Answers—Exercise #1B—Case

Our Test Review Was a Game!

Mr. Bogosian tried something new in class today: he played a review
   1. us   *2. We*
game to give <u>we</u> a chance to get ready for our test. <u>Us</u> kids actually had fun playing the game. Francisco answered the most questions so
   3. him
we clapped for <u>he</u>. Even so, we were the real winners since more than half of us earned our best test score of the year.

Explanations of Answers

1. The object pronoun **"us"** is correct since it is the indirect object.
2. The subject pronoun **"We"** is correct since it is used in the subject position.
3. The object pronoun **"him"** is correct since it is the object of the preposition **"for."**

©Copyright 2008 by Barron's Educational Series, Inc.

Answers—Exercise #1C—Gender

1. Mrs. Cairo asked Mary to pick up (**her**, its) books.
2. Jackson took (**his**, its) brother to the movies.
3. The table can hold (her, **its**) own weight.

Explanations of Answers

1. The correct answer is "**her**" since Mary is a girl.
2. The correct answer is "**his**" since Jackson is a boy.
3. The correct answer is "**its**" since the table is neutral: neither a girl nor a boy.

TARGET SKILL 2: MISPLACED MODIFIERS

Answers and Explanations

1. A suggested answer is "**In her desk, Savannah found a lady's blue bracelet.**" The bracelet is blue, not the lady.
2. A suggested answer is "**I once met a one-armed man named Rashawn.**" The man is named Rashawn, not his arm.
3. A suggested answer is "**I heard on the evening news that the burglar has been captured.**" The evening news is the place where the news was heard, not the location where the capture took place.

TARGET SKILL 3: VOICE

Answers and Explanations

1. A suggested answer is "**Students filled every desk in the library yesterday.**" The students do the action in an active voice sentence.
2. A suggested answer is "**At my favorite ice cream store, the new owner prepared my sundae.**" The new owner is doing the action.
3. A suggested answer is "**My parents scolded me when I didn't do all my chores yesterday.**" The parents are doing the scolding.

TARGET SKILL 4: SENTENCE VARIETY

Answers

The following is one sample of the way this paragraph could have used more sentence variety.

Answer Keys and Explanations

Getting in Trouble

1. 2.
Yesterday I unexpectedly got into some trouble. My friends and I forgot our manners,
3.
and we cut across our neighbor's lawn. He became very upset, and then he started
4. 5.
yelling at us. We tried to explain to him that we weren't hurting anything. He said that
6.
somebody stole his lawn chair as a prank. Now he's blaming us, even though we're
7.
innocent. I guess we shouldn't have walked on his lawn.

Explanations of Answers

1. Change the position of the adverb **"Yesterday"** and add the word **"unexpectedly."**
2. Change the sentence to a compound sentence.
3. Combine the next two sentences into a compound sentence.
4. Change the simple sentence into a complex one (**". . . that we weren't hurting anything"** can't stand alone as a sentence because of the word **"that"**).
5. No change was made.
6. Combine the next two sentences to make a complex sentence.
7. No change was made.

(Remember that these changes are suggestions. Your answers may be different.)

TARGET SKILLS 5 & 6: FRAGMENTS AND RUN-ONS

Answers #5—Fragments

1. A suggested answer is "My cousin and I walked through the park."
2. A suggested answer is "My best friend from Vineland is visiting me today."
3. A suggested answer is "Exercising every morning keeps me in shape."

Answers #6—Run-ons

1. A suggested answer is "Come to my birthday party because it will be fun."

©Copyright 2008 by Barron's Educational Series, Inc.

2. A suggested answer is "Because I'm doing my homework now, I can't talk to you."
3. A suggested answer is "I'll take out the trash, and then I'll walk the dog."

TARGET SKILLS 7 & 8: PUNCTUATION WITH COMMAS AND END MARKS

Answers #7—Commas

1. I had a hamburger, and you had pizza.
2. My mom asked me to go to the store, mail a letter, and put my dirty clothes in the wash.
3. Because I earned all "A's" and "B's" on my report card, I'm getting a reward.
4. We moved to New Jersey from Springfield, Ohio.
5. "Sincerely yours, Allen" is the ending I used for my letter.
6. No, I won't make fun of the new student in our class.
7. The winner of the fund-raising challenge was Nicole, a student from my class.

Answers #8—End Marks

1. I just won a million dollars! (Exclamatory Sentence)
2. Please take care of yourself. (Imperative Sentence)
3. Did you eat the last piece of cake? (Interrogative Sentence)
4. The class project will be due on March 3. (Declarative Sentence)

TARGET SKILLS 9 & 10: HOMOPHONES AND HOMOGRAPHS

Answers #9—Homophones

1. The correct answer is **"sew,"** which means to use "a needle and thread to join together cloth or other similar material." The homonym **"so"** means "thus" or "therefore."
2. The correct answer is **"They're,"** which is the contraction of "They are." **"Their"** is a pronoun showing ownership by more than one person, and **"There"** refers to a direction that is usually not close by.
3. The correct answer is **"to,"** which is a preposition usually meaning a direction. **"Too"** means "also," and **"Two"** is the number following one.
4. The correct answer is **"hear,"** which means receiving communication through the ear. **"Here"** means a nearby location.
5. The correct answer is **"flower,"** which is the blossom of a plant. **"Flour"** is grain that is very finely milled (ground).

Answers #10—Homographs

1. The correct answer is "B. The covering of a tree."
2. The correct answer is "A. Not heavy."
3. The correct answer is "A. Admirer."
4. The correct answer is "B. Skin cut."
5. The correct answer is "B. Happening in the present time."

TARGET SKILL 11: GRAMMAR DEMONS

Answers #11A—Unusual Order

1. The correct answer is "**are**" because the subject is "**tickets.**"
2. The correct answer is "**is**" because the subject is "**outfit.**"
3. The correct answer is "**is**" because the subject is "**rip.**"
4. The correct answer is "**are**" because the subject is "**gloves.**"

Answers #11B—Adjective or Adverb

1. The correct answer is **"good"** because this adjective modifies the noun **"meal."**
2. The correct answer is **"well"** because we are referring to health.
3. The correct answer is **"bad"** because this adjective modifies the noun **"meal."**
4. The correct answer is **"badly"** because this adverb modifies the verb **"performed."**
5. The correct answer is **"really"** because this adverb modifies the adjective **"good."**
6. The correct answer is **"real"** because this predicate adjective follows the linking verb **"is"** and modifies the subject **"wish."**

Answers #11C—Quotations

1. The correct answer is: "The principal said over the intercom, "Students, please report to the cafeteria at the end of second period today."
2. The correct answer is: "Write your homework assignment in your notebooks," said Mrs. Hudson.
3. The correct answer is: "Are we there yet?" said my brother after every five minutes of our trip.
4. The correct answer is: "Should we go to the park?" said Carrie, "or should we go to the ball field?"
5. The correct answer is: I answered, "We should go to the park. They're having a special program there. Besides, all our friends will be there too."
6. The correct answer is: "That's sounds great!" said Carrie.

©Copyright 2008 by Barron's Educational Series, Inc.

Answers #11D—Underlining or Quotation Marks

1. The correct answer is: My sister is reading <u>Great Expectations</u>, a novel by Charles Dickens.
2. The correct answer is: In class we read "Dream Deferred," a poem by Langston Hughes.
3. The correct answer is: Before the play-off game, we stood and took off our caps as the loudspeakers played "God Bless America."
4. The correct answer is: In class today, Mr. Porter read an article from <u>The New York Times</u>.

Target Skill 12: Spelling Demons

1. The correct answer is "If you don't bring a note to excuse your absence from school, you'll get a detention."
2. The correct answer is "Let's buy some balloons for our party."
3. The correct answer is "I am assigned the job of changing the date on the class calendar."
4. The correct answer is "The month after January is February."
5. The correct answer is "Do we have any grammar homework tonight?"
6. The correct answer is "Oops, my shoelaces are loose."
7. The correct answer is "Our town's parade occurred last weekend."
8. The correct answer is "Mom asked me to get the butter for the mashed potatoes."
9. The correct answer is "Our music class is studying rhythm and blues artists from the 1970's."
10. The correct answer is "I used the vacuum to pick up the dirt that spilled on the rug."

CHAPTER 6

PRACTICE TEST 1

PART 1—Writing

Writing Task A—Persuasive Letter

February 25, 2008

Dear Dr. Byrnes,

   I am writing this letter to you to share my opinion about the state department of education's proposal to make us an online school. I think that having an online school may seem to be a great idea, but I myself have some reservations. Classes on the Internet might be interesting, but there would be less focus on the lesson, less direct contact with the teachers and students, and less opportunity for our school to function as classes and teams.

I think the biggest drawback is the lack of focus in an online school. Teenagers enjoy learning in a classroom where they can be with their friends. It is not the same to watch a monitor and "experience" a class without any friends around to help them to pay attention to the lesson. A virtual classroom that can be held anywhere holds a potential for distraction with music videos, instant messages, phone calls, Internet "surfing", and even parents and siblings providing distraction. In a classroom, we students have both the teacher and our friends to remind us to pay attention. In an online classroom, we have to rely on our own self-discipline. Remember, we are teenagers. It would be very easy for us to "tune out" the lesson that's being broadcast to our homes.

The next problem is similar to the first one. By reducing the contact between students and the teacher, there are few opportunities for a personal education. Rather, the lessons are pre-made and completely student-directed. This may be fine for the students who don't get along well in school, but it would be a disaster for those of us who enjoy having heated discussions about issues that matter. In fact, how can an online school know that we students may be having a problem on a particular day, and we really need to have a caring teacher listen to us and give us some feedback? No Internet search can provide us with that personal touch.

Finally, an online school disregards the importance of teams. Many of the projects that we do in our classes are team projects. I have learned to plan my work in advance, cooperate with my teammates, help a teammate who may be struggling, and even go to my team if I'm having a problem. These skills are the ones we will need when we grow up and live in a society that values teamwork, cooperation, good planning, support, and the need for close relationships with families and friends. Throughout my eight years in our schools, I have made three best friends as a direct result of being a teammate in my classes. Moreover, Mrs. Antonini has been one of my greatest supporters since I became a member of her debate team in fifth grade.

Dr. Brynes, please reconsider the school's decision to become an online school. I am sure that the state department of education is trying to improve our learning opportunities, but I think they are wrong this time. They are creating a system that will challenge us to focus on our lessons. In addition, they are giving us less contact with our valued teachers and friends while preventing us from acquiring team building skills that are so important for our future success.

Thank you for your time and consideration. I will gladly meet with you if you wish to discuss my letter further.

Sincerely,
Jennifer Marie Cromartie

Explanation of Grade

This letter is probably going to receive a grade of "5" or "6." The question has been answered thoroughly. The author begins by stating the main point clearly at the beginning of the letter: "I am writing this letter to you to share my opinion about the state department of education's proposal to make us an online school." She makes three points and develops each in its own paragraph. She supports her first point ("the lack of focus in an online school") with statements about not having "friends around" to help her friends and her "to pay attention," using "A virtual classroom" that "holds a potential for distraction," and needing "to rely on our own self-discipline." The remaining points are similarly supported. There is insight when she mentions that "It would be very easy for us to 'tune out' the lesson that's being broadcast to our homes" an online school lacks "that personal touch," and the friends she has made "as a direct result of being a teammate in my classes." Finally, her essay uses correct grammar, spelling, and vocabulary. Notice that there are no contractions used in a formal piece of writing.

Writing Task B—Speculative Essay

This picture has a roller coaster in it. Two people was sitting in the front, and two people was sitting behind them. The kids look happy. So does the adults.

The two kids went to go to the amusement park, but the boy was afraid to go on the roller coaster. His sister axed him to go on with her, but he says he was sick and wanted to go home. She says that he didn't look sick when they were on the spinning tea cups ride, but he says he was sick. So he wanted to go home. Now.

His sister says "OK." He said "OK" too. But then she says what's wrong and he didn't answer. So she asked him again and he says he was afraid. So she said she would go on the ride with him. He said "OK."

So they went on the ride. And they had a good time.

Explanation of Grade

This answer would probably receive a low score of "1" or "2." The writer did use paragraphs and even attempted to use dialogue. There is a plot, but it is not very well developed. There is no title for the story. The characters are not given an age or a personality. In fact, they're not even given a name. The response is very short in length. There are also grammar errors. In the first paragraph, "was" should be "were" and "does" should be "do." In the second paragraph, "axed" should be "asked." In the second and third paragraphs, "says" should be "said." The word "Now" is not a sentence. In the third paragraph, "But" and "So" should not begin sentences. In the third and fourth sentences, there should be a comma before "and" since the sentences would be compound if they didn't start with "But" and "So." In the fourth paragraph, "So" and "And" should not begin sentences.

The author needs to add more details to the story. The characters should have names, and their personalities and feelings should be mentioned (nervous, frustrated, and courageous, for example). The plot needs more details, which can be found in the conflict. The reader can easily give the young boy in the story a reason for being afraid of the roller coaster ride. Maybe the boy had a bad experience on the ride the last time he visited the amusement park. Some meaningful dialogue could help the reader to understand the young boy's fear of the roller coaster.

To conclude the story, the author should do two things. First of all, (s)he should describe the actual ride so the reader will be able to see that the brother's fears are going away. Second, (s)he should have the brother and sister both reflect on the change in attitude that has occurred. The brother's conquering of his fear has taught him a lesson: It may be difficult, but it is always necessary to face one's fears.

PART II—READING NARRATIVE

Multiple-Choice Answers

1. C 2. D 3. A 4. B 5. C 6. D 7. B 8. B 9. A 10. C

Short Essay—Sample Answer

This fable is created around a conflict. The carefree Grasshopper is "hopping about, chirping and singing to its heart's content" while the serious Ant, is "lay(ing) up food for the winter." When the Ant recommends that the Grasshopper do "the same," the Grasshopper ignores the advice. When winter comes, the Grasshopper is found to be "dying of hunger" as he learns "It is best to prepare for the days of necessity."

Explanation of Grade

This essay should receive a grade of "3." It directly addresses the conflict of the fable, and it states the resolution clearly. Quotes including the Grasshopper's "hopping about, chirping and singing to its heart's content" and the Ant's "lay(ing) up food for the winter" are used. Finally, there are no grammar or spelling mistakes.

Long Essay—Sample Answer

If the Grasshopper wrote the fable, he'd be the man! The Ant would forget about work and join in the summer fun. They could still do a little work, too. You know, all work and no play makes yuh dull and borring. Besides, why didn't the ants share their food with him? They had enough. He said he would share his fun with them in the summer. How come they won't help him out now? I just don't get it!

Explanation of Grade

This essay should receive a grade of "1" or "2." It directly answers the question, but it does so with slang: "he'd be the man!" The author does use supporting details ("The Ant would forget the work" and the Grasshopper said "he would share his fun with them in the summer"). Even so there should be additional ones dealing with the change to the Grasshopper's point of view. For example, he would see the Ant's refusal to "forget the work" as being shortsighted and silly. He probably would even scold the Ant for not taking his (the Grasshopper's) advice. The phrases "You know" and "I just don't get it!" are too informal. Any insight in the statement about the Grasshopper sharing "his fun" is lost in the conversational tone. The answer is very brief. Finally, there are two spelling mistakes ("yuh" instead of "you" and "borring" instead of "boring") and one grammatical one ("all work and no play 'makes' instead of 'make'").

©Copyright 2008 by Barron's Educational Series, Inc.

PART III—INFORMATIONAL READING

Multiple-Choice Answers

1. A 2. C 3. C 4. D 5. B 6. C 7. A 8. B 9. D 10. D

Short Essay—Sample Answer

If they Oakville Middle School Field Trip notice change to a short storie, dat's dum. Nobody want tuh reed dat. I reed a book wit a short storie once. It's goofy.

Explanation of Grade

This essay should receive a grade of "0." It avoids rather than addresses the question being posed. There are no supporting details and no insight. The author should have mentioned the need for at least one main character, a plot featuring one or more actions on the field trip, a conflict, and some rising action that leads to a resolution. There may have also been dialogue. Furthermore, the language in the response is simplistic. There are two grammar mistakes ("notice" instead of "notices" and "want" instead of "wants"). The spelling mistakes include "they" instead of "the," "storie" instead of "story," "dat's" instead of "that is," "dum" instead of "dumb," "tuh" instead of "to," "reed" instead of "read," "dat" instead of "that," "wit" instead of "with," and "storie" instead of "story." Also, the phrases "dat's dum," "Nobody want tuh reed dat," and "It's goofy" demonstrate poor and inappropriate vocabulary choices, as well as misspellings.

Long Essay—Sample Answer

If the Oakville Middle School Field Trip notice were written as a diary entry, there would definitely be some changes made. A diary is personal; a field trip notice is not. A diary gives the writer's personal feelings about people, events, or situations. Every action being portrayed in the diary would therefore be seen directly through the writer's eyes. The main focus of the piece would not be the details of the trip to the Elmore Kicks Soccer Stadium and the Thrills Amusement Park. Rather, it would be the author's report of his/her time spent during the trip. The rules and guidelines may or may not be considered to be important. The importance of these rules would depend on the way they might affect the author.

The information being reported in the diary would likely change from fact to opinion. A diary is written to give an author's impression of a certain event. This diary may or may not include the general success of the trip, depending on the intent of the author. There would likely be a mention of at least one other student, who might be either a close friend or adversary, as well as the author's impression of the major events of the day.

Explanation of Grade

This essay should receive a grade of "4." It states the difference between a diary and a field trip notice ("A diary is personal; a field trip notice is not. A diary gives the writer's personal feelings about people, events, or situations.") even before it directly answers the question. Supporting details are stated clearly ("The main focus of the piece would not be the details of the trip to the Elmore Kicks Soccer Stadium and the Thrills Amusement Park. Rather, it would be the author's report of his or her time spent during the trip."). The topic is covered completely and with insight ("Every action being portrayed in the diary would therefore be seen directly through the writer's eyes," "The importance of these rules would depend on the way they might affect the author," and "This diary may or may not include the general success of the trip, depending on the intent of the author."). The vocabulary is appropriate ("portrayed" instead of "written about" and "adversary" instead of "enemy"), and the grammar and spelling are correct.

PRACTICE TEST 2

PART 1—Writing

Writing Task A—Persuasive Essay

NO UNIFORMS IN PUBLIC SCHOOLS

There's no weigh all public school students should hafta wear uniforms. It takes away our individuality, it's expensive, and some kids could be allergic to them. The choice should be upto us students.

Part of the fun of being a teenager is being an individual. We like to dress up in clothes that show how we feel that day. We like to show off our latest fashions. Some of us get clothes on our birthdays, but now we won't get them. Instead, we'll probably get books or backpacks. Hooray!

Buying school uniforms is expensive. Some kids can't afford to buy more than two sets of clothes that they can't wear any place else but at school. Our parents work hard to earn their money, and they won't be able to buy us a lot of new clothes. And what about the parent who's out of work? What do they do when their kids need new uniforms?

Wearing these uniforms is also a problem for another reason. They are hot, and some kids are allergic to the fabrics the uniforms are made from. What do they do? If they don't wear the uniforms, they can't come to school. If they don't come to school, they'll get in trouble. If they do come to school in their regular clothes, they'll also get in trouble. That's not fair since these kids didn't ask to be allergic to the uniforms.

We should be allowed to wear our own school clothes, not uniforms that somebody picks out for us. If a kid is going to do well in school, the uniform won't make any difference. It's the kid's effort that matters.

Explanation of Grade

This essay is probably going to receive a grade of "2" or "3." The question has been answered somewhat thoroughly, but the thoughts are mostly obvious ones. The author should focus more on the point of dressing in clothes that are stylish and flattering to the student's shape and preferences. The simple way that the sentences are written in the first paragraph hurts the author's chances right from the beginning, along with the three spelling mistakes ("weigh" instead of "way," "hafta" instead of "have to," and "upto" instead of "up to"). There are supporting details, but the test reader will be "put off" by

the comment in paragraph two that states "Some of us get clothes on our birthdays, but now we won't get them. Instead, we'll probably get books or backpacks. Hooray!" Some insight is seen in the comments about the "out of work" parents who mazay be having difficulty buying uniforms for their children and the problems for "kids (who) are allergic to the fabrics the uniforms are made from." This last phrase should use correct grammar by referring to "the fabrics **from which** the uniforms are made."

Writing Task B—Speculative Essay

DEALING WITH TROUBLE

Kareem had just moved into Lakeview when he first met the boy everyone called "Trouble." Kareem would soon learn that by using his head, he could actually solve a major problem being caused by Trouble.

It seems that one sunny afternoon, Kareem planned to go to the local park. He had heard that there was a nice basketball court there for all the kids in town to use. "Maybe I can find a game and play on one of the teams," he thought to himself. "I used to be a pretty good player at Mountain Hills, my old school. I really miss my old friends."

Since Kareem had just moved into his new house on Friday, he wouldn't be going to school until Monday. He was more than a little bit upset that he had to leave all of his best friends at Mountain View. He wasn't sure how long it would take to make some new friends at Lakeview School.

Before going outside, Kareem asked his mom, "Couldn't we have moved here a few days sooner so I could have made some new friends at school?"

Kareem's mom replied, "You know we couldn't leave any earlier. Things just didn't work out that way. Besides, you can make some new friends very easily. Why don't you go down to that nice park we passed on the way to our new house?"

"That's exactly where I'm heading," Kareem told his mom.

"Remember to be home for dinner," said Kareem's mom.

He answered, "I will," and he went outside.

As soon as Kareem had reached the end of the block, he looked up and saw the meanest-looking kid he had ever seen. Kareem felt a little bit afraid, but he didn't run away. That would only make this new kid chase after him.

Kareem walked up to the new kid and introduced himself. When he asked the kid for his name, the kid snarled, "Trouble—you got a problem with that?"

Kareem thought to himself, "Only one day, and I'm already having problems." Kareem thought about trying to be nice to the kid, but he had tried that once with a mean kid back home and the kid started to hit him. What could he do?

In an instant, Trouble stood right in front of Kareem. They were face to face. Trouble started to scream at Kareem, and now Kareem really wanted to run away. Yet, he knew that he couldn't run because Trouble would then bully him for a long, long time.

Finally, Kareem remembered what his older cousin Saleem had told him. Saleem had said, "Kareem, don't ever let someone bully you. If you let them do this once, it will just be worse every time."

Even so, Kareem didn't want to fight. He was taught as a little kid only to fight if there were no other possible way to stop a bully. "I guess I have no choice," thought Kareem to himself. "I'm going to have to fight Trouble."

Trouble pushed Kareem hard, and Kareem started to lose his balance. Trouble then called Kareem a weakling. Even worse, Trouble was taunting Kareem to take the first swing at him.

Just then, Kareem got an idea. "What if I stand up to him by telling him I'm not afraid? I'll tell him that I'll fight him if I have to, but I really don't dislike him. Would Trouble be surprised? More importantly, would he leave me alone? I guess it's worth a try."

With that, Kareem stood up and told Trouble that he would fight him if he had to. Even so, he preferred not to fight Trouble because he really didn't dislike him. Besides, he wasn't even angry with Trouble.

For a moment, Trouble screamed at Kareem, his voice getting louder and louder. Yet, Kareem refused to fight, although he did worry that his plan might backfire. "What if Trouble gets angry and starts to beat me up? What will I do?" he wondered to himself.

Then, for some reason, Trouble just stopped screaming at Kareem. Trouble had a puzzled look on his face. Remember, Kareem wasn't screaming insults at Trouble. Instead, Trouble was the one doing all the screaming.

Trouble was so surprised that he started to laugh. All the meanness was gone from his face. For the first time, he actually looked like a regular kid and not a bully.

Trouble smiled at Kareem and said, "Hey, kid, that was pretty smart. You know, you're not like the other kids around here. They would have run away or tried to fight me. You used your brain. That's pretty sharp, kid."

Kareem answered, "Thanks, but you shouldn't try to scare people the way you tried to scare me. It's not very nice. Plus, you might just meet somebody who could beat you up. Then what would you do?"

"I don't know. It's never happened before," stated Trouble.

Kareem asked Trouble, "Hey, do you wanna shoot some hoops?"

Trouble looked down and said, "I don't know how."

"C'mon, I'll teach you," said Kareem, "and I promise I won't laugh at you if you mess up."

"Really?" said Trouble. "It's a deal."

The two boys took a leisurely stroll to the park. This day didn't start out very well for Kareem, but it really had improved in a short time. Kareem didn't expect any more trouble for the rest of the day.

Explanation of Grade

This answer would probably receive a high score of "5" or "6." The writer used a clever title that summarized the conflict and story line: "Dealing with Trouble." The plotline is foreshadowed in the second sentence: "Kareem would soon learn that by using his head, he could actually solve a major problem being caused by Trouble." Details about the character Kareem are shared with the reader almost immediately. The author states that Kareem was "a really good player" at Mountain Hills, his former school. Kareem "was more than a little bit upset that he had to leave all of his best friends at Mountain View." He learns that there is "a nice basketball court" at the local park, and Kareem hopes to "find a game and play on one of the teams."

The conflict that Kareem must try to resolve is not uncommon—everyone has had to face a bully at one time or another. Kareem's method was to stand up to Trouble instead of trying to fight him. The resolution of the two boys becoming friends shows that Kareem did learn how to deal with trouble effectively, as the author states in the title.

The grammar, spelling, and word selection in the story reflect a higher level of writing. For example, the compound sentence "Kareem felt a little bit afraid, but he didn't run away" contains a comma before the word "but." Slang expressions like "wanna" and "C'mon" are used only conversationally. The sentences are written in varying lengths and styles. Some begin with the subject and verb first ("Kareem had just moved into Lakeview …"). Others begin differently ("In an instant, Trouble stood right in front of Kareem."). The compound sentences are punctuated correctly ("Kareem felt a little bit afraid, but he didn't run away" and "This day didn't start out very well for Kareem, but it really had improved in a short time."). Concerning word selection, the author used words like "introduced" instead of "met up with" and "taunting" instead of "bothering."

The author used two types of dialogue. The first is the regular type between the two characters. The conversation between Kareem and his mom and the conversations between Kareem and Trouble are both examples of the effective use of dialogue. The author has also used inner dialogue throughout the work to give the reader direct access to Kareem's thoughts. An example of inner dialogue is, "Kareem thought to himself, 'Only one day, and I'm already having problems.'"

PART II—READING NARRATIVE

Multiple-Choice Answers

1. A 2. B 3. D 4. B 5. C 6. A 7. C 8. D 9. B 10. C

Short Essay—Sample Answer

Kipling is advising his son about the ways to act in a mature manner. He tells him, "If you can wait and not be tired by waiting, / Or, being lied about, don't deal in lies, / Or being hated don't give way to hating, / And yet don't look too good, nor talk too wise". Not being "tired by waiting" displays patience. Kipling's advice not to "deal in lies" when you are "being lied about" shows his son that telling the truth is important. We can't control what others say, but can surely control what we say. Not hating others who hate us further demonstrates maturity. Finally, not looking "too good" or talking "too wise(ly)" means not acting in a superior way to others.

Explanation of Grade

This essay should receive a grade of "2." It directly answers the question by pointing out that "Kipling is advising his son about the ways to act in a mature manner." The author then explains each line by citing quotes from the text. For example, he states that "Not being 'tired by waiting' displays patience." The author also adds insight by explaining the meaning of each quote. The opening line about "advising his son" demonstrates the need "to act in a mature manner." The final sentence talks about the maturity behind "not acting in a superior way to others."

Long Essay—Sample Answer

If the poem were being written as a news story, it would be very different. The last line of the poem, "you'll be a Man, my son," would actually be included at the very beginning of the story. News stories are written with the most important information first. As the story moves on, the information becomes less and less critical.

The author would rephrase all the statements beginning with the word "If." In fact, only a few of them would be used since other information would need to be included. The five "W's" (Who? What? When? Where? and Why?) and one "H" ("How?") would need to be included. Otherwise, the story would not be a true news story. For example, the names and possibly ages of the father and son would be given, the name of the town or city would be stated, and the time of the event would be reported. There would probably be quotes from the father and the son, along with those from friends or neighbors who are connected to the event. Furthermore, the rhymes including "you" and "too" and "lies" and "wise" would not be seen in a news report but possibly in a song about the event. Finally, the story would be written in paragraphs and not stanzas.

Explanation of Grade

This essay should receive a grade of "4." It directly addresses the question in the opening sentence when the author states, "If the poem were being written as a news story, it would be very different." It uses supporting details by giving reasons for each point. For example, in a news story "the names and possibly ages of the father and son would be given, the name of the town or city would be stated, and the time of the event would be reported." There are other supporting details including "the use of the five "W's" and one "H," the use of quotes, the elimination of rhyme, and the use of paragraphs in place of stanzas. The second line of the essay displays insight when the author says, "The last line of the poem, 'you'll be a Man, my son,' would actually be included at the very beginning of the story." Finally, the grammar, spelling, and vocabulary are appropriate and correct.

PART III—INFORMATIONAL (EVERYDAY) READING

Multiple-Choice Answers

1. B   2. C   3. D   4. A   5. B   6. C   7. A   8. D   9. A   10. C

Short Essay—Sample Answer

Two major changes take place in skateboarding from the 1950's to the 1970's. These deal with the equipment used by the skaters. First of all, the composition of the wheels changes. The clay wheels used in the 1950's cause problems because they "break down quickly and don't have the proper grip." In the 1970's, these clay wheels are replaced by those made from urethane ones, which last longer and grip better. Secondly, the decks of the boards in the 1970's are widened to give skateboarders "more control and maneuverability" than they had in the 1950's. These and other improvements helped to increase the popularity of skateboarding.

©Copyright 2008 by Barron's Educational Series, Inc.

Explanation of Grade

This essay should receive a grade of "2." It thoroughly answers the question by restating it in the first sentence and then giving the necessary details from the text. The author not only gives the changes ("the composition of the wheels" and widening "the decks of the boards"), but also gives the impact of the changes (urethane wheels "last longer and grip better" and wider decks provide "more control and maneuverability"). Insight is added with the statement, "These and other improvements helped to increase the popularity of skateboarding." There are no spelling or grammar mistakes. The vocabulary choices are appropriate. For example, the author uses the word "composition" to describe the material of the wheels and the word "improvements" instead of the phrase "things that make it better."

Long Essay—Sample Answer

Skateboarding has risen in popularity. This began in the 1990's with good stuff happening. The Extreme games were held, bringing, the sport to everybody, the boards were made better since they were "more stable and easier to control," and safety is better. More skateparks were even being built.

In the 2000's, most boards are put together with "seven laminated sheets of Canadian maple wood" and wheels improved. Pro boarders are finally getting sponsorships, and kids are playing video games. Avril Lavigne sings "Sk8er Boi." Danny Way makes a big jump in China. Skateboarding might even become an Olympic sport. Yeah, skateboarding is becoming more awesome everyday.

Explanation of Grade

This grade for this essay is probably a "3." The question is answered somewhat thoroughly with a lot of supporting detail. The author uses information from the 1990's to show how it leads into the information from the 2000's. The staging of the Extreme Games is mentioned, but ESPN is not. The improvement in the boards ("more stable and easier to control") uses a citation from the text as support, and the rise in both safety and the number of skateparks is noted. The information from the 2000's cites board composition ("seven laminated sheets of Canadian maple wood"), wheel improvement, and the rise in sponsorships and video games. Also mentioned are Danny Way's jump and Avril Lavigne's song, but the interest from the Olympics is omitted. There is some insight, but it is phrased poorly. "Yeah, skateboarding is becoming more awesome everyday," the final statement of the essay, is non-specific and slang. The spelling is precise. This is especially seen in the title "Sk8ter Boi." There is one grammar mistake: the phrase "The Extreme games were held, bringing, the sport . . ." should be written without the comma after bringing. The vocabulary is above average, but the phrases "good stuff" and awesome" are slang.

Chapter 9: APPENDIX

SUCCESS TIPS FOR NJ ASK7 LAL ESSAY WRITING

- Write clear and precise topic sentences.
- Organize your thoughts before you begin to write. Use bullet points, a graphic organizer, an outline, or any type of organizer to help you.
- Have a clear idea of your essay's main points before you begin writing.
- Practice persuasive writing and all your writing skills regularly and often. Always write clearly and with focus. Otherwise, you may be practicing the wrong skills. The saying **Practice makes perfect** should be **Perfect practice makes perfect**.
- Read material at your reading level to help you to be a better writer. Your mind will learn what good writers do to make their points clearly and specifically. Reading these skilled authors will actually help you to be a better writer.
- When you practice your writing, share your drafts with a skilled friend and a trusted adult who are good writers and editors. They can give you the feedback that you need to improve your writing skills.
- Read your practice drafts out loud after you write them so your mind and your brain can both hear your essay. If possible, have someone read your drafts out loud to you. You'll get feedback from your reader while you listen to your writing from a comfortable *distance*. You may find mistakes that you might have missed if you had only read your drafts silently. You may even read your essay into a recorder and then listen to it "on tape."
- Be specific. Your readers only know what you're telling them.
- Try proofreading your drafts by reading them backwards. This works best when you check for mistakes with spelling and the use of homophones (words that sound alike but have different spellings, meanings, or origins, like *blue* and *blew*). This strategy doesn't work for content, logic, or grammar, however.
- Begin practicing for the NJ ASK Language Arts Literacy Test for Grade 7 as soon as possible. The sooner you begin, the sooner you can practice writing for success.

TEST-TAKING SUCCESS STRATEGIES

PREPARING AHEAD FOR THE TEST

- Review your skills.
- Study alone so you can concentrate on your work.
- Study with serious friends who want to study.
- Practice with the type of problems that you will be facing on the test.
- Pay close attention to the test reviews in your classroom.
- Write down information that you learn for the first time and then review it over the next few days.
- Stay aware of the time it takes you to complete your review exercises in class. If you cannot finish on time, ask your teacher for some help.

PREPARING THE NIGHT BEFORE THE TEST

- Get enough sleep—not too much or too little.
- Don't worry about the test. It's important, but it should not frighten you.
- Avoid cramming for the test. This will only tire you out and hurt your performance on the actual test the next day.
- Set your alarm to wake-up early enough to have breakfast.

GETTING READY ON THE MORNING OF THE TEST

- Wake up early enough so you don't have to start off the day by rushing.
- Avoid arguing.
- Have a good breakfast, but don't overeat.
- Leave for school a few minutes early so you can deal with any problems that might arise.
- Don't spend your morning worrying about the test.

TAKING THE TEST

- Read all directions and follow all instructions.
- Look only at your paper and no one else's.
- Plan your time wisely so you won't have to rush or leave sections incomplete.
- Use all the strategies that you have learned.
- Do the most difficult questions in a section first. Then answer the rest.
- If you skip a question, make sure you skip to the next answer space.
- Proofread your writing.
- Make sure your multiple-choice questions are answered in the correct spaces.
- Avoid changing answers. Your first impression is usually correct.

SAMPLE GRAPHIC ORGANIZERS
PERSUASIVE ESSAY FLOW CHART

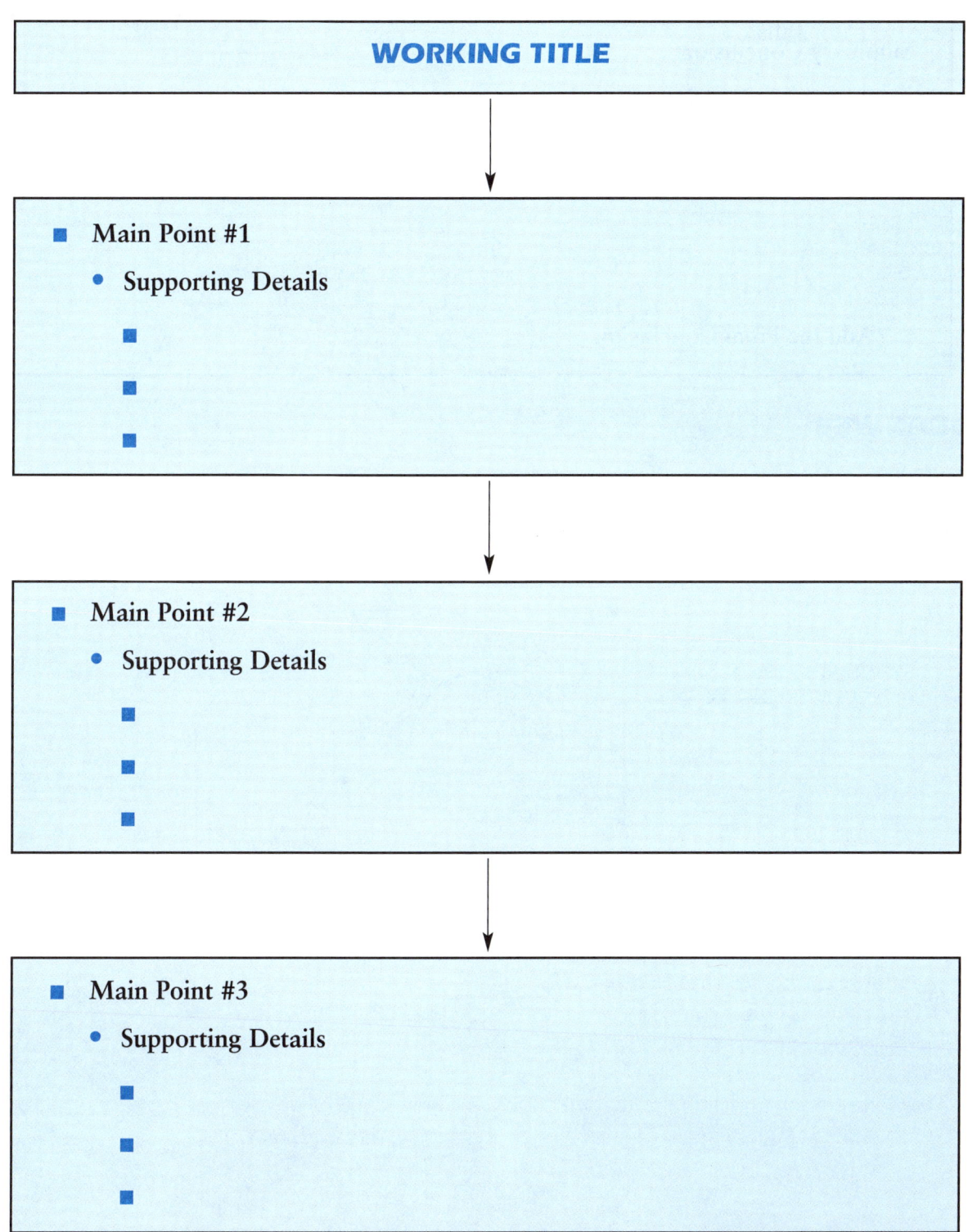

Summary Conclusion

- Restate the Thesis (Main Idea).
- Restate the Three Main Points.
    -
    -
    -
- Add the Final Conclusion.

IDEAS WEB

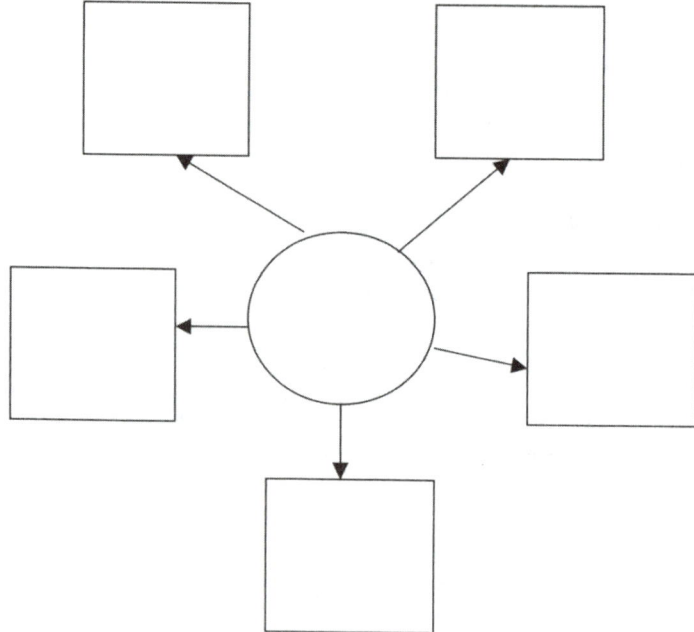

COLUMN CHART

Title	
Main Point #1	Supporting Details
Main Point #2	Supporting Details
Main Point #3	Supporting Details

IDEAS PIZZA—BEST FOR BRAINSTORMING

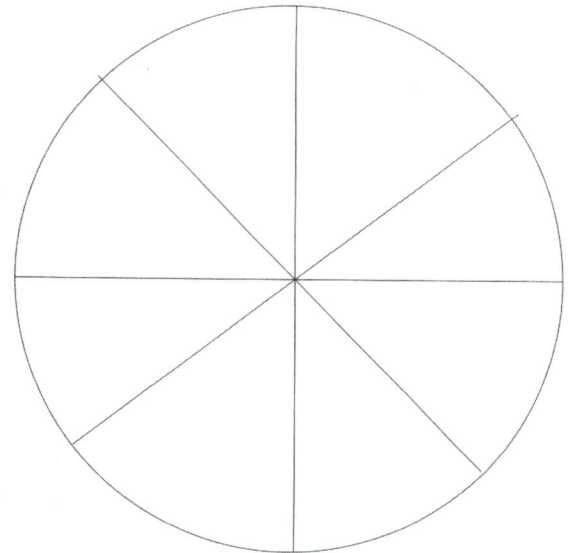

SPECULATIVE WRITING ORGANIZATION SHEET

Step #1—Create the Realistic Main Conflict
Step #2—Create the Plot (Plan of Action)
Step #3—Create the Setting
Step #4—Give Each Main Character a Personality
Step #5—Develop the Story (Plot Line)
Step #6—Write the Solution for the Problem (Resolve the Conflict)
Step #7—Give Your Story a Working Title
Step #8—Write Your First Draft
Step #9—Add Dialogue
Step #10—Edit & Submit Your Essay

SOME COMMONLY MISSPELLED WORDS

1. absence
2. abundance
3. accessible
4. accommodate
5. achieve
6. advice/advise
7. appearance
8. amateur
9. argument
10. attendance
11. balloon
12. belief/believe
13. business
14. calendar
15. cemetery
16. changeable
17. conscience
18. consistent
19. deceive
20. dependent
21. dilemma
22. discipline
23. embarrass
24. exceed
25. February
26. fiery
27. foreign
28. forty
29. government
30. grammar
31. guidance
32. heroes
33. hygiene
34. independence
35. irresistible
36. knowledge
37. license
38. manufacture
39. maintenance
40. millionaire
41. miniature
42. mathematics
43. mischievous
44. misspell
45. neighbor
46. occasion
47. occurrence
48. parallel
49. pleasant
50. precede
51. prejudice
52. principal/principle
53. pursue
54. recommend
55. reference
56. restaurant
57. rhythm
58. secretary
59. seize
60. sergeant
61. shepherd
62. sincerely
63. strength
64. studying
65. syllable
66. synonym
67. technique
68. tragedy
69. twelfth
70. unnecessary
71. vacuum
72. villain
73. Wednesday
74. weird
75. yacht